A
DAILY GUIDE
to
KNOWING GOD

A Daily Guide to Knowing God

LUD GOLZ

TYNDALE HOUSE PUBLISHERS, INC.
WHEATON, ILLINOIS

Library of Congress Catalog Card Number 78-66371
ISBN 0-8423-0510-6, paper
Copyright © 1978 by Lud Golz. All rights reserved.
First printing, November 1978
Printed in the United States of America.

INTRODUCTION

Freedom!

Why is it so elusive?

Many, if not most, live as though imprisoned. Never really confident to be themselves. Never daring to become all they were meant to be. Always hiding behind a mask which restricts and distorts.

We all need release. We need to be set free! But how?

Jesus declared, "If you abide in My word, then you are truly disciples of Mine; and you shall know the truth, and *the truth shall make you free!*" (*John 8:31, 32*).

A Daily Guide to Knowing God is a manual with daily readings designed to be catalysts for meditation and worship based on biblical truth. The primary thrust is doctrinal. Anecdote and illustration are deliberately limited. The objective is to use the Bible references and the author's thoughts as springboards to meditation and worship.

Integrated into the daily sequence are readings designed to motivate you to read through the Bible in a year. The first such reading is January 2. You will find indicated how many days it should take to read through Genesis—fifteen days, January 2 through January 16. If you follow this guide you will discover Exodus introduced on January 17, with a similar suggestion of eleven days to read it. If you follow these suggested time allotments for reading each book of the Bible you will read through the Bible in a year. Do it in conjunction with the daily readings in this manual.

During the final two months you'll find some simplified Bible study methods that can help you learn the discipline and delight of feeding yourself from the rich storehouse of God's Word.

I pray that every daily reading will help you build on what has gone before so that on this "truth journey" you will experience your own journey into freedom through knowing God.

Lud Golz
Novelty, Ohio

Dedicated to my mother,
whose prayer ministry
has undergirded my life
and ministry.

1 JANUARY

"In the beginning God" (Genesis 1:1)

If you want to experience life as it ought to be, you must allow God to be first in your thoughts. He was before all things. He had no beginning. He is the uncreated Creator of all things and beings.

I am a fool if I think or say, "There is no God" (*Psalm 14:1*). Life is meaningless without Him.

It is a comfort and a challenge when facing obstacles or opportunities, temptations or tragedies, to think about the fact that no matter what happens, God is there. You can always turn to Him and experience the wonderful truth that He cares for you (*1 Peter 5:7*). But when you turn to Him you must believe that He is and that He is a rewarder of those who diligently seek Him (*Hebrews 11:6*).

Faith in the existence of God is basic to Christianity and is the foundation for this book. It is fundamental if you want a fruitful and fulfilling life.

2 JANUARY

TAKE THE LONG LOOK—GENESIS (fifteen days to read)

"And as for you, you meant evil against me, but God meant it for good in order to bring about this present result, to preserve many people alive" (Genesis 50:20).

"Oh no! I knew this would happen."

Have you ever said this in an attitude of disgust when everything just seemed to go wrong? I have. But while reading Genesis I discovered a wonderful truth: God is involved in the events of my life. He providentially governs and guides men and their circumstances to fulfill His purposes. This is seen in the life of every major character in the book of Genesis—in the whole Bible for that matter.

Joseph is but one example. In his life almost everything
went wrong. He, however, believed God would work it all
out for good in the end. He was not disappointed. Nor will
we be, if we learn to have confidence that God will fulfill
His purpose and plan in our lives even when things seem to
go wrong. Take the long look by trusting God to care for
you.

3 JANUARY

*"In the beginning God created the heavens and
the earth" (Genesis 1:1).*

Heaven and earth are not eternal. They had a beginning.
They were not formed from some substance which was
eternal. They were created out of absolutely nothing. When
Moses penned these words he did not intend for them to be
merely a heading or summary statement of creation.

The creation of the heavens and the earth is in fact the
beginning of all things material and spiritual, except God.
Because the Hebrew language offered no single word to
identify the universe, Moses used the expression "the
heavens and the earth."

In our future home in heaven, a prominent theme of
worship will be "Thou art worthy, O Lord, to receive glory
and honor and power: for thou hast created all things, and
for thy pleasure they are and were created" (*Revelation 4:11,
KJV*). This is also a legitimate theme of worship for each of
us to use daily. Never forget that we as His creation are to
please Him in all we do.

4 JANUARY

"In the beginning God created . . ."
(Genesis 1:1).

God alone is eternal. Though "the heavens are telling of
the glory of God; and the firmament is declaring
the work of His hands" *(Psalm 19:1)*, we must never
worship these as though they were God or even a part of
God. That is idolatry. True worship is directed toward the
Creator, not toward what He has created.

God created out of nothing the matter which He used to
creatively form the things and beings which did and do
exist. It is proper to conclude that I am a product of God's
creation and, therefore, am responsible to Him. My proper
position is that of submission and dependence. Independence is the root of all man's trouble.

It is with this in mind that Peter says, "Let those also
who suffer according to the will of God entrust their souls
to a faithful Creator in doing what is right" *(1 Peter 4:19).*

5 JANUARY

"In the beginning was the Word . . . the
Word was God . . . the Word became flesh"
(John 1:1, 14).

Here we have a series of statements identifying "the
Word" with what is said in Genesis 1:1, "In the beginning
God." "The Word was God." Not "a god," as some have
attempted to translate falsely. "The Word became flesh."
Quite obviously if you read the entire portion in John's
Gospel, "The Word" is none other than the historical per-
son, Jesus Christ.

"The Word" was God before He became flesh. When He
became flesh, however, He did not become something less

than God. In a unique way Jesus Christ was the God-Man, fully God and fully man. Paul says, "For in Him all the fulness of Deity dwells in bodily form" (*Colossians 2:9*).

Paul wrote to the Philippians, "Christ Jesus, who has always been and at present continues to subsist in that mode of being in which He gives outward expression of His essential nature, that of absolute deity, which expression comes from and is truly representative of His inner being (that of absolute deity), and who did not after weighing the facts, consider it a treasure to be clutched and retained at all hazards, this being on an equality with deity (in the expression of the divine essence), but himself He emptied, himself He made void, having taken the outward expression of a bondslave, which expression comes from and is truly representative of His nature (as deity), entering into a new state of existence, that of mankind" (*Philippians 2:6, 7, The New Testament: An Expanded Translation*, Wuest).

6 JANUARY

"In the beginning was the Word . . . All things came into being through Him; and apart from Him nothing came into being that has come into being" (*John 1:1, 3*).

Jesus Christ, "the Word," as God, was the Creator of all that is—"the heaven and earth." Together with the Father, He determined what was to be, and then He brought them into being. My world is the product of His creative act. I also came into being through Him. I am His by creation. Any time I go my own way, to do my own thing, independent of Him, I am violating the law of creation. He once said, "Apart from Me you can do nothing" (*John 15:5*). I am dependent upon Him if I am to realize His purpose for me. I am responsible to Him. He deserves my allegiance and my worship.

"In Him all things were created, both in the heavens and on earth, visible and invisible, whether thrones or dominions or rulers or authorities—all things have been created through Him" (*Colossians 1:16*). "And, Thou, Lord, in the beginning didst lay the foundation of the earth, and the heavens are the works of Thy hands" (*Hebrews 1:10*).

7 JANUARY

"In the beginning was the Word, and the Word was with God, and the Word was God" (*John 1:1*).

We have already established the truth that Jesus Christ, "the Word," was and is God. As you consider this first verse in John's Gospel, it is clear that two personalities are in focus: "The Word," who is God, and God. Does this contradict the Old Testament teaching that "The Lord is our God, the Lord is one!" (*Deuteronomy 6:4*)?

No. We read, "Then God said, 'Let *us* make man in *our* image, according to *our* likeness . . .' And God created man in *His* own image" (*Genesis 1:26, 27*). Here we have the plural "us" and "our" together with the singular "His," all referring to God. God is one in essence but plural in personality. He has eternally been that way.

Another reference pointing this out is Isaiah 6:8, where God says, "Whom shall *I* send, and who will go for *us*?" Jesus once said, "I and the Father are one [a unity or one essence]" (*John 10:30*).

8 JANUARY

"All things have been created through Him and for Him" (*Colossians 1:16*).

Creation is the result of action taken by Jesus Christ.

That action was taken to make something for Himself. As God, He did not need what He created. He simply chose to make it.

It was made for Him in the sense of providing pleasure. Satisfaction comes when one is able to see the work of His hands and enjoy it. Creation was made for Christ also in the sense of being responsible to Him. It was made to glorify Him. When what is created responsibly fulfills its designated objective, He who created it is glorified.

Jesus Christ is now sitting at His Father's right hand waiting for "the summing up of all things in Christ, things in the heavens and things upon the earth" (*Ephesians 1:10*). This summing up refers to a regathering or restoring to a state which once was true within all of creation. There was originally a harmony of all things to the will and pleasure of God. He said of all He had created, "It is good." Satan's rebellion in heaven and man's sin on earth brought a curse. Christ took the full brunt of the curse on Himself at the cross and triumphed over it. Now He awaits the day when the ultimate effect of His triumph will be felt by all things created being restored to acknowledging His authority.

9 JANUARY

"The eternal Spirit" (Hebrews 9:14).

We have observed that two persons of the Godhead existed before anything was made. Now we look at the third person of the Godhead, the Holy Spirit, and we see that He also is eternal. Being eternal, He was not created. It is proper to say, "In the beginning was the Holy Spirit."

Since existence without having a beginning is a characteristic of God, the Holy Spirit is God. He is of the same divine essence as God the Father and God the Son. Yet He is as distinct a person within the Godhead as the Father and the Son.

Peter told Ananias and Sapphira that they lied to the Holy Spirit regarding their offering to the church in

Jerusalem. Then he explained that this was a serious act because they did not lie just to men, but to God (*Acts 5:1-11*). According to Peter, the Holy Spirit was God. We are to reverence the Holy Spirit even as we do Jesus Christ and God the Father. They are the one Lord.

10 JANUARY

"The Spirit of God has made me" (Job 33:4).

Opinions differ on whether Genesis 1:1 and Genesis 1:2 refer to the same period of time—"In the beginning." Some feel that in verse 1 God created a perfect heaven and earth. Then, when Satan rebelled against God and led a revolt with some of the angels, God disrupted what He had made, and the earth became formless and void (verse 2). God then recreated or reformed what was into what is described in Genesis 1 and 2.

Others feel that in verse 1 God created matter out of which He formed the earth. Then He progressively developed it as described in Genesis 1 and 2.

Either way, the Bible declares that the Holy Spirit was a participant in the act of creating, and this is an act of God. "And the Spirit of God was moving over the surface of the waters" (*Genesis 1:2*). "Thou dost send forth Thy Spirit, they are created" (*Psalm 104:30*). "By his Spirit he hath garnished the heavens" (*Job 26:13, KJV*).

11 JANUARY

"God said, 'Let us make man in our image, according to our likeness'" (Genesis 1:26).

All things were created by God, each in its order and

according to its kind. The highest created being on the earth was man, created in the image of God. Since God is Spirit, man's likeness to him is not physical. Even as my shadow is a likeness of me, it is not the same as me. The Hebrew word for *image* is the word used for *shadow*. By looking at man, one can gain something of an understanding of what God is like.

Paul suggests what that likeness involves when he says, "Put on the new self, which in the likeness of God has been created in righteousness and holiness of the truth" (*Ephesians 4:24*). And, "Put on the new self who is being renewed to a true knowledge according to the image of the One who created him" (*Colossians 3:10*). Man was created a moral and rational creature. He knows the right and good. He has the ability to understand, evaluate, relate, and develop ideas. He has free will and self-consciousness. God made man capable of knowing Him and having communion with Him.

12 JANUARY

"And God created man in His own image, in the image of God He created him" (Genesis 1:27).

We have seen that man was created with a moral and intellectual likeness to God. This is further substantiated by the fact that whatever beast or fowl God brought to him, Adam gave it a name (*Genesis 2:19*). Also, he was given the right and responsibility to subdue the earth and to have dominion over every living thing upon the earth (*Genesis 1:28*).

Many would try to refute this by postulating that man evolved from a lower order of being, over extensive periods of time. Not only does the Bible contradict such a postulate; history itself contradicts it. It is pseudo-science which demands such a conclusion. If anything, man has degenerated over the years—especially in the area of morals.

Given sufficient time, man will destroy himself and all that's living around him, if God does not restrain and intervene.

13 JANUARY

"Male and female He created them" (*Genesis 1:27*).

According to Genesis God began with creating Adam (*Genesis 2:7*). He then created a garden into which He placed Adam. In God's judgment, Adam needed a helper. So God put Adam to sleep, took one of his ribs from his side, and out of it formed a suitable helper. Adam called this helper, Woman, "because she was taken out of man" (*Genesis 2:23*).

Man and woman were so compatible that by mutual consent they could become "one flesh" (*Genesis 2:24*). And through their relationship they could reproduce themselves, bearing children in their own likeness, according to their image (*Genesis 5:3*).

The order which God established between man and woman is clearly set forth in the Bible. "I want you to understand that Christ is the head of every man, and the man is the head of a woman . . . For man does not originate from woman, but woman from man; for indeed man was not created for the woman's sake, but woman for the man's sake . . . However, in the Lord, neither is woman independent of man, nor is man independent of woman. For as the woman originates from the man, so also the man has his birth through the woman; and all things originate from God" (*1 Corinthians 11:3-12*).

14 JANUARY

"The enemy . . . is the devil"(Matthew 13:39).
We have seen that to live properly we must
have faith in God. God must come first in every area of our
life. Jesus said, "Seek first His kingdom, and His
righteousness; and all these things [daily necessities] shall be
added to you" (*Matthew 6:33*). You will find, however,
when you set out to do this in your life that there is one
who will do all he can to oppose you. That enemy is the
devil!

The Bible refers to the devil as a personal being, with
great power and craftiness. He is more than man can handle
with his own wisdom and strength. In fact, everyone in the
world who has not been delivered through faith in Christ is
presently in the hand and under the control of the devil
(*1 John 5:19*).

Anyone in a battle must know and believe in his enemy if
he is to win the battle. The Bible identifies your spiritual
enemy so you can wage a winning battle against him.

15 JANUARY

*"In Him all things were created, both in the
heavens and on earth, visible and invisible,
whether thrones or dominions or rulers or authorities"*
(*Colossians 1:16*).

Our enemy, the devil, likely one of the highest of created
beings, did not maintain the proper attitude of reverence
and submissive obedience to the eternal Creator, God. Many
feel that the prophet Isaiah is not only referring to the king
of Babylon he describes in Isaiah 14, but that beginning
with verse 12 he is referring to the devil as originally
created: "O star of the morning, son of the dawn." His
description continues by showing that this beautiful,
glorious creature had free will, which he used to rebel

against God: "You said in your heart, *I will* ascend to heaven; *I will* raise my throne above the stars of God . . . *I will* make myself like the Most High" (verses 13, 14). God overthrew that rebellion and cast the devil down to the earth (verse 12) and to "Sheol, to the recesses of the pit" (verse 15). Likely, the prophet Ezekiel also referred to the devil when he described the king of Tyre in Ezekiel 28:12-17.

16 JANUARY

"Now the serpent was more crafty than any beast of the field which the Lord God had made. And he said to the woman, 'Indeed, has God said . . . ?'" (Genesis 3:1).

All that God created was good as it came from His hand. Even the serpent. Why would the devil choose the serpent for his nefarious act? Because shrewdness was a natural characteristic of the serpent (*Matthew 10:16*). Shrewdness is not wrong unless used in a deceitful way. The devil provided the deceit.

Through the serpent, the devil first cast doubt on what God had said by exaggerating His prohibition (*Genesis 3:1;* compare *2:16, 17*). He followed up with a direct challenge to the truthfulness of God (verse 4), and a veiled lie about God's motive for giving the prohibition (verse 5). What he said in verse 5 did indeed happen to Adam and Eve when they disobeyed God. They did become "like God, knowing good and evil." But the truth in that statement was cunningly designed to cover up the lie in verse 4: "You surely shall not die!" Jesus says of the devil, "He is a liar, and the father of lies" (*John 8:44*). Beware of his wiles!

17 JANUARY

OUR DELIVERANCE—EXODUS (eleven days to read)

"But Moses told the people, 'Don't be afraid. Just stand where you are and watch, and you will see the wonderful way the Lord will rescue you today. The Egyptians you are looking at—you will never see them again. The Lord will fight for you, and you won't need to lift a finger'" (Exodus 14:13, 14, The Living Bible).

No one likes to be caught in the middle of difficulties. At times, however, it's the best thing that could happen to us. God often leads us right into such circumstances. Why? To teach us of His power to deliver. When you read Exodus you'll see this portrayed vividly in Israel's deliverance from bondage.

Israel's exodus, however, was followed by tragedy. They did not continue to believe God's power to deliver was available for their daily needs. They grumbled when they should have given thanks.

We must learn that God will lead us into victory at all times when we rely on Him continually and give thanks in all things.

18 JANUARY

"The woman . . . took from its fruit and ate; and she gave also to her husband with her, and he ate" (Genesis 3:6).

"As distrust of God's command leads to a disregard of it, so the longing for a false independence excites a desire for the seeming good that has been prohibited; and this desire is fostered by the senses, until it brings forth sin. Doubt, unbelief, and pride were the roots of the sin of our first parents, as they have been of all the sins of their posterity."[1]

Man, created in God's image, was uniquely qualified to have fellowship with God. But by using his free will, he followed the cunning lies of the devil into disobedience. He wanted, even as the devil had wanted, to be like God.

The desire for independence from God and from His will is sin. And the consequence of sin is death. "In the day that you eat from it you shall surely die" *(Genesis 2:17)*.

As Paul the apostle scans human history, he concludes, "Just as through one man [Adam] sin entered into the world, and death through sin, and so death spread to all men, *because all sinned . . ." (Romans 5:12)*.

1. *Carl F. Keil and Franz Delitzsch, Old Testament Commentaries, Vol. 1 (Grand Rapids: Eerdmans, © 1971), pp. 95, 96. Used by permission.*

19 JANUARY

"The heart is deceitful above all things, and desperately wicked: who can know it?"
(Jeremiah 17:9, KJV).

Most of us do not think of ourselves as desperately wicked. That's because we have been deceived by our own hearts and don't really know ourselves. Paul, in the book of Romans, presents the lost condition of all men in the first two chapters and then summarizes the verdict as follows:

"As the Scriptures say, 'No one is good—no one in all the world is innocent.' No one has ever really followed God's paths, or even truly wanted to. Every one has turned away; all have gone wrong. No one anywhere has kept on doing what is right; not one. Their talk is foul and filthy like the stench from an open grave. Their tongues are loaded with lies. Everything they say has in it the sting and poison of deadly snakes. Their mouths are full of cursing and bitterness. They are quick to kill, hating anyone who disagrees with them. Wherever they go they leave misery and trouble behind them, and they have never known what it is to feel secure or enjoy God's blessing. They care nothing about God nor what He thinks of them.

"So the judgment of God lies very heavily upon the Jews, for they are responsible to keep God's laws instead of doing all these evil things; not one of them has any excuse; in fact, all the world stands hushed and guilty before Almighty God. Now do you see it? No one can ever be made right in God's sight by doing what the law commands. For the more we know of God's laws, the clearer it becomes that we aren't obeying them; His laws serve only to make us see that we are sinners.

"But now God has shown us a different way to heaven— not by 'being good enough' and trying to keep His laws, but by a new way (though not new, really, for the Scriptures told about it long ago). Now God says He will accept and acquit us—declare us 'not guilty'—if we trust Jesus Christ to take away our sins. And we all can be saved in this same way, by coming to Christ, no matter who we are or what we have been like.

"Yes, all have sinned; all fall short of God's glorious ideal; yet now God declares us 'not guilty' of offending Him if we trust in Jesus Christ, who in His kindness freely takes away our sins" (*Romans 3:10-24, The Living Bible*).

20 JANUARY

"For the wages of sin is death, but the free gift of God is eternal life in Christ Jesus our Lord" (*Romans 6:23*).

There is no way for man to experience eternal life as a result of his own efforts. Being a sinner, even our good actions are like filthy rags (*Isaiah 64:6*). Man, if left to himself, is without hope (*Ephesians 2:12*). Death, both spiritual and physical, is his lot. And in the end, he will be consigned to what the Bible calls the lake of fire, which is the second death (*Revelation 20:14*).

"But the free gift of God is eternal life in Christ Jesus our Lord." There is no greater message nor better news. Man can't earn eternal life, nor merit it. Man doesn't deserve it. God, out of the goodness of His heart, offers man eternal life as a free gift. All man can do is receive it by faith. This is why the Psalmist says, "Salvation comes from God" (*Psalm 3:8, The Living Bible*).

"For by grace you have been saved through faith; and that not of yourselves, it is the gift of God; not as a result of works, that no one should boast" (*Ephesians 2:8, 9*).

21 JANUARY

"As you therefore have received Christ Jesus the Lord, so walk in Him" (*Colossians 2:6*).

We enter into the family of God and become Christians through receiving the gift of eternal life in Jesus Christ. It is by faith that we receive the gift. An emotional experience may accompany this decision to receive, but it is not essential. All that is essential is an awareness that we are sinners, separated from God by our sin and because of our sin, and a decision by faith to turn from ourselves to the Savior, Jesus Christ. Jesus said He would never reject anyone who came to Him (*John 6:37*).

Once you have taken that step of coming to Jesus Christ, you are to continue walking in Him. How do you do that? If you could not save yourself, do you think you can live as a saved person should live by your own efforts? Never. It took faith in Jesus Christ to become saved. It likewise takes faith in Jesus Christ to walk in Him and for Him. Without Him you can do nothing. But Paul could say, "I can do all things through Him who strengthens me" (*Philippians 4:13*).

"Now who is it that continues to conquer the world, if it is not the person who [continuously] believes that Jesus is the Son of God" (*1 John 5:5, Williams*).

22 JANUARY

"I will build My church" (*Matthew 16:18*).

The word for church comes from *ek*, out of, and *klesis*, a calling. It was used among the Greeks to designate a gathering of citizens called together for any purpose. When used regarding the Christian church it has two applications: 1) the total company of Christians throughout the period of grace; that is, from the time of Pentecost till Christ returns; 2) a group of Christians banded together in a given local area.

When Jesus said, "My church," He was referring to the whole company of the redeemed throughout the present age. They are all persons whom He has called out of the grip of the wicked one and made His own. That which makes them the company or the Church of Jesus Christ is their common experience of salvation. No matter what church affiliation someone might have, or whether he has any affiliation, if he has trusted in Jesus Christ for his salvation, he is a member of "My church"—that is, the universal Church of Jesus Christ. Jesus Christ is building His Church throughout the world today. Are you a member of His Church?

23 JANUARY

"I will build My church (*Matthew 16:18*).

Only God could speak with the ring of certainty found in these five words. That which started as just a handful of followers quickly developed into an army of Spirit-filled disciples who were referred to by their enemies as those who have filled Jerusalem with their teaching (*Acts 5:28*). And again, as those who have "turned the world upside down" (*Acts 17:6, KJV*).

This growth and outreach is the direct result of the promise made by Jesus Christ, "I will build My church." As is true of the individual Christian's growth, the growth of the corporate body of Christians constituting the Church is accomplished only through Jesus Christ. Without Him we can do nothing (*John 15:5*).

The building materials for this spiritual building are less than desirable. In fact they are rejects (*Romans 7:18*). But when the Master Builder takes over, He erects a building of rare beauty and eternal stability.

"You also, as living stones, are being built up as a spiritual house for a holy priesthood, to offer up spiritual sacrifices acceptable to God through Jesus Christ" (*1 Peter 2:5*).

24 JANUARY

"I will build My church; and the gates of Hades [hell] shall not overpower it" (*Matthew 16:18*).

There is no question about the fact that Jesus Christ will build His Church. There is a question in the minds of some as to whether or not the archenemy of Jesus Christ will be able to overpower and overthrow the Church. Many attempts have been made both by subversive elements within the churches and destructive opponents outside them. At times it has seemed that the flickering light of truth was almost dispelled. Always, at the right time, God had his man or woman through whom He rekindled the flame.

In our own day, as we approach the climax of human history, the powers of evil are running rampant throughout the world. Who would have thought that civilized people would be so gullible and so easily led into darkness? Even many Christians are found dabbling curiously into the intriguing world of the forbidden fruit. "The gates of Hell" are unleashing their fiercest attack. But in the face of all this foreboding darkness, rest assured; what Jesus Christ promised will be fulfilled. The Church He is building will triumph. Praise His name!

25 JANUARY

"But we do not want you to be uninformed, brethren, about those who are asleep [dead], that you may not grieve, as do the rest who have no hope" (1 Thessalonians 4:13).

A common experience is to have a troubled heart when thinking about a loved one's death or your own death. The Christian should not have a troubled heart when contemplating death. Nor should he be troubled by the death of another believer. Death is not the end. There is more. "For if we believe that Jesus died and rose again, even so God will bring with Him those who have fallen asleep in Jesus" *(1 Thessalonians 4:14)*.

Our confidence for the future is based upon the promise of Jesus Christ that He will return to take to Himself all who have trusted in Him for salvation. Someone has calculated that Christ's return is mentioned 318 times in the 260 chapters of the New Testament—once in every twenty-five verses. His return is the blessed hope of every believer. Read John 14:1-3 for the exhilarating confidence Jesus wants us to enjoy about life beyond the grave.

26 JANUARY

"We who are alive, and remain until the coming of the Lord" (1 Thessalonians 4:15).

Death is not the end for the Christian. That's why we need not sorrow as those without hope. When Christ returns for His own, those who are dead in Christ will rise first (*1 Thessalonians 4:16*).

Many believers will be alive when the Lord comes. They too will be remembered by the Lord. One condition is no better than the other. The Christian professes with the psalmist, "My times are in Thy hand" (*Psalm 31:15*). He knows "it is appointed for men to die once" (*Hebrews 9:27*). The fear of death has no grip on him for he knows that Jesus Christ became a man "that through death He might render powerless him who had the power of death, that is, the devil" (*Hebrews 2:14, 15*).

The whole Church, consisting of all who have through the years put their faith in Jesus Christ for salvation, will be caught up to meet the returning Lord in the air. This grand exodus is the final stage of the "calling out" process begun by our Lord. "The Lord knows those who are His" (*2 Timothy 2:19*). Not one will be missing on that day. Amen.

27 JANUARY

"We shall always be with the Lord" (1 Thessalonians 4:17).

The order of *that* day is as follows: "The Lord Himself with a cry of command, with an archangel's voice, and with a call of a trumpet sounded at God's command, shall descend from heaven, and the dead in Christ shall be raised first, then as for us who are living and who are left behind, together with them we shall be snatched away forcibly in (masses of saints having the appearance of) clouds for a welcome—meeting with the Lord in the lower atmosphere.

And thus always shall we be with the Lord. So that—be
encouraging one another with these words" (*1 Thessalonians 4:16-18, Wuest*).

The "cry of command" and the "call of a trumpet" are
for the saints to hear. This exodus or *rapture* will be secret
so far as the world is concerned. It will come as a surprise to
them. What explanations they will give for the missing is
unknown. What will happen to vehicles driven or airplanes
piloted by Christians at the moment of the rapture is known
only to God. The fact remains—those who know God
through faith in Jesus Christ will be missing on the earth.
What a shattering experience for those who knew of God's
promise but because of unbelief will still be here—*lost*.
What a joy it will be for believers to be with Him whom
they have loved in this life. Let this glorious truth both
challenge and comfort your heart.

28 JANUARY

GOD'S DEMANDS—LEVITICUS
(eight days to read)
*"Thus you are to be holy to Me, for I the Lord am holy;
and I have set you apart from the peoples to be Mine"*
(*Leviticus 20:26*).

Man was created to be at peace with God and have
fellowship with Him. God has a plan for our lives, but we
rebelled and went our own way (*Isaiah 53:6*). This is sin and
it is what separates us from God.

Leviticus tells us how seriously God considers our sin to
be. Nothing short of a blood sacrifice will take sin away.
The temple ritual is described in detail, teaching us that we
must take care how we approach a holy God. Carelessness
in worship is dangerous.

The sacrifices and the temple ritual are a picture which
looks forward to Jesus Christ and what He would do for us
through the sacrifice of Himself on the cross. We need

forgiveness and cleansing from our sin. His blood sacrifice alone can do this for us.

By faith we must confess our sin and trust in His sacrifice to have peace and fellowship with God.

29 JANUARY

"We must work the works of Him who sent Me, as long as it is day; night is coming, when no man can work" (John 9:4).

Christ is coming soon. Those who are prepared will rejoice on that day. But those who are not prepared face the sad prospect of being eternally separated from the presence of God.

As long as it is day, we should work as hard and efficiently as possible. No sacrifice should be considered too great to get the job done of telling the good news of Christ's salvation to all men. There are *opportunities everywhere* as long as it is day. But the longer you put your work off, the more your *opportunities ebb away.* When night comes your *opportunities will end*—"no man can work."

If you are going to reach anyone with the good news, you must do it *now.* Never take the luxury of putting off for tomorrow what you can do today. Our mission is not a game. Eternity is at stake. Priceless lives for whom Christ died are at stake. Let us not fail to fulfill our appointed task.

At the end of His earthly life, Jesus said to His Father, "I glorified Thee on the earth, having accomplished the work which Thou hast given Me to do" (*John 17:4*).

30 JANUARY

"Go therefore and make disciples of all the nations" (Matthew 28:19).

The command is not "to go," but "to make disciples." The verse can be correctly translated, *"As you go*, therefore, make disciples . . ."* When persons truly understand and experience the good news of eternal and abundant life through Jesus Christ they will go out into their world to share what they have found with others. Going is the natural result of receiving.

The reason many professing Christians do not go forth with the good news is that they are anemic. Either they don't understand the implications of receiving Christ as Lord or they have reneged on their commitment. Possibly they are ignorant of the enabling provision God has made for them to do His work.

There is more to our mission, however, than merely sharing what we have found. We are to communicate what we have found in such a convincing and clear way that our hearers will respond to the Savior and become followers of Jesus Christ. Making sure they understand the implications of Christ being Lord of their lives is a part of the process of making disciples. Another part is to follow up their commitments in order to observe their behavior, encourage their growth, and correct their failures. This constant watchcare is essential for laying a strong foundation upon which a strong life can be built. As Dr. Malcolm Cronk says, "It takes time for a babe in Christ to become a man of God."

31 JANUARY

"Go therefore and make disciples of all the nations" (Matthew 28:19).

Our task is not done until there are those from "all the nations" who name the name of Jesus Christ and follow

Him as their Lord. In fact, John prophetically describes a scene in which the Lamb of God is proclaimed as worthy to "take the book, and to break its seals; for Thou wast slain, and didst purchase for God with Thy blood men from every tribe and tongue and people and nation" (*Revelation 5:9*).

All believers are to be witnesses to their neighbors. They are always to be ready to give an answer to every man who asks them for a reason for the hope which is within them (*1 Peter 3:15*). *Some* believers are specially singled out by God the Holy Spirit, and sent forth to the yet unreached peoples of the world to tell them the good news. What a joy when the church is enjoying such close fellowship that when the Holy Spirit calls one to such a mission the whole church senses what He is doing and cooperates in sending him forth (*Acts 13:1-3*). What have you and your church done to see this great mission accomplished? What could you do to help in a greater way?

1 FEBRUARY

"Before the mountains were created, before the earth was formed, you are God without beginning or end" (Psalm 90:2, The Living Bible).

God was before time. God will be after time. God is above time. With God there is no sequence of events or experiences. God sees everything in the eternal present. God is not limited by time as we are. We are given seventy years as our lifetime (*Psalm 90:10*), and what a mess we make of the opportunities that are ours. God has eternity and His ways are all perfect.

When God called Moses to lead Israel out of Egyptian bondage, Moses wanted to know what he should say when the Israelites ask him, "Who sent you? What is His name?" God's answer was, "I AM WHO I AM . . . Thus you shall say to the sons of Israel, 'I AM has sent me to you'" (*Exodus 3:13, 14*).

Names were always important in biblical times. Names revealed character. When God revealed His name "I AM" to Moses, He was declaring that He is/was/always shall be self-existent, not dependent upon any other person or thing. He is eternally complete in Himself. This One, who did not need us but desired us, created us capable of fellowship with Him, not only for time but for eternity. Don't neglect that fellowship potential. Cultivate it daily.

2 FEBRUARY

"For I, the Lord, do not change" (Malachi 3:6).

Every day we awaken to a changing world. The new world becomes the old world so rapidly that many people find no security in the world of their experience. It is so easy to be "conformed to this world" (*Romans 12:2*) or "pressed into the mold of this world," as J. B. Phillips puts it. Money, position, possessions, education, health—all promise security, but the events of a single day can remove any one of those security blankets, leaving your life shattered and storm tossed if you have put all your hope in such transitory things.

If you want security, turn to and trust in the Lord God *who changes not. He is immutable.* Were He to change, He would not be God. The statement, "I know not what the future holds, but I know who holds the future," is meaningful only if God is unchanging. I have confidence of forgiveness only if God is unchanging in His ability to forgive. All that is promised in God's Word is certain only if God is unchangeable. Let us, together with James, praise "the Father of lights, with whom there is no variation, or shifting shadow" (*James 1:17*).

"God also bound himself with an oath, so that those he promised to help would be perfectly sure and never need to wonder whether he might change his plans. He has given both his promise and his oath, two things we can completely count on, for it is impossible for God to tell a lie. Now all those who flee to him to save them can take new courage when they hear such assurances from God; now they can know without doubt that he will give them the salvation he has promised them. This certain hope of being saved is a strong and trustworthy anchor for our souls" (*Hebrews 6:17-19, The Living Bible*).

3 FEBRUARY

"The Glory of Israel [God] will not lie or change His mind [repent]; for He is not a man that He should change His mind" (1 Samuel 15:29).

How is one to understand this declaration of God's unchangeableness when in other places Scriptures (such as Jonah 3:10) indicate that God did repent?

If you consider the historical context of the Jonah reference you will find that God remained the same in character. He always hates sin and must judge it. He always delights in seeing His creatures walking in humble obedience before Him. As people or nations change in their attitude or conduct He must change His response to them. Nineveh was a stench to God's nostrils because of their sinfulness, and God pronounced judgment. When they repented and humbled themselves before God, He responded to this change by forgiving and withdrawing His promised judgment.

God's dealings with humans change only as they change in their attitude and conduct. The unchanging character of God actually is substantiated by His changing His response to our changes.

This is further substantiated by looking at subsequent history. Ninevah later reverted to her sinful ways. Light received increases light; light rejected brings night. Nineveh's rebellion and rejection of light brought upon her the horrible night of God's judgment described in the book of Nahum.

4 FEBRUARY

"God is not a man, that He should lie, nor a son of man, that He should repent; has He said, and will He not do it? Or has He spoken, and will He not make it good?" (Numbers 23:19).

Good men keep their word. At least they try to. At best every good man has failed at one time or another in keeping his word. Not necessarily because he wanted to, but because circumstances at times are such that man is incapable of keeping his word.

God is never limited or boxed in like that. He doesn't have to lie to get out of a difficult situation. When He speaks, He does what He says. He always makes good on His word.

Sometimes man's conduct is such that God must adjust His approach. Genesis 6:6 (KJV) says, "And it repented the

Lord that He had made man on the earth, and it grieved Him at His heart." We have already considered what is involved when God repents. When He must repent because of man's sin, it grieves Him deeply. But it doesn't cause Him to fail regarding His word. He knows a way and is capable of carrying it through. He never fails.

5 FEBRUARY

GOD IS NOT IN A HURRY—NUMBERS
(eleven days to read)

"God is not a man, that He should lie, nor a son of man, that He should repent; has He said, and will He not do it? Or has He spoken, and will He not make it good?" (Numbers 23:19).

The late president of Wheaton College, Dr. V. R. Edman, used to say, "Never doubt in the dark what God has told you in the daylight." Israel did. And their doubt and consequent disobedience brought delays in the fulfillment of God's plan for their lives.

The book of Numbers reveals God's patience in executing His plan. Nothing could frustrate Him. Israel complained, rebelled, and disobeyed, but God still fulfilled His promise. How? By active involvement. When Israel sinned He stopped and dealt with them. Patiently, step by step, He led them on.

We must learn that God is never in a hurry. When we disobey He directs the process of our lives through the fiery furnace of circumstances. Through those circumstances He removes the impurities. Then He starts us off again from where we went astray. And the experience makes us better persons. Oh, the wisdom and patience of God!

6 FEBRUARY

"Jesus Christ is the same yesterday and today, yes and forever" (Hebrews 13:8).

Jesus Christ is the eternal Son of God. He is referred to as "God blessed forever" *(Romans 9:5)*. He refers to Himself as "The Alpha and the Omega, the first and the last, the beginning and the end" *(Revelation 21:13)*. The Bible declares that Jesus Christ had no beginning, was not created, and will have no ending. This attribute of being eternal is true only of God. In this, He is one with the Father.

"With reference to Christ, the phrase 'the only begotten from the Father' *(John 1:14)*, indicates that as the Son of God He was the sole representative of the being and character of the One who sent Him. He is not merely making a comparison with earthly relationships. The glory was that of a unique relationship, and the word 'begotten' does not imply a beginning of His Sonship. It suggests relationship indeed, but must be distinguished from generation as applied to man."[2]

2. William E. Vine, *An Expository Dictionary of New Testament Words, Vol. 3 (Old Tappan, N.J.: Revell, © 1940), p. 140. Used by permission.*

7 FEBRUARY

"No man hath seen God at any time; the only begotten Son, which is in the bosom of the Father, he hath declared him" (John 1:18, KJV).

We can rightly understand the term "the only begotten" when used of the Son, only in the sense of unoriginated relationship. A devout scholar, Bishop Moule, put it this way: "The begetting is not an event of time, however remote, but a fact irrespective of time. The Christ did not become, but necessarily and eternally *is* the Son. He, a Person, possesses every attribute of pure Godhood. This necessitates eternity, absolute being; in this respect He is not 'after' the Father."[3]

References to Jesus Christ being the only begotten Son (such as *John 1:18; 3:16; 3:18*) suggest the intimacy of His eternal relationship with the Father—an intimacy in which they experienced each other's love, enjoyed each other's thoughts, and exemplified the ultimate harmony. Jesus Christ did not become the only begotten son when given to be the Savior. The inestimable value of God's love gift is in that the Father gave the eternal, unique Son. Only as such could Jesus fully reveal the character and will, love and grace of His Father and therefore become the only valid object of our faith.

3. *Ibid.*

8 FEBRUARY

"Before Abraham was born, I AM" (John 8:58).

It is obvious that in His discussion with the Jews referred to in John 8:48-59, Jesus was saying, "I am God." That is why they took up stones to throw at Him. They felt He was blaspheming God.

He used the same designation for Himself as God used when talking to Moses. "I AM" indicates that He is a person, that He is self-existent, changeless, eternal. *He had changed* in His outward manifestation from that of glory to that of servitude, from heavenly to earthly. He had taken upon Himself the veil of humanity. He was God eternally. He became the God-Man at a point in time. He remained changeless, however, in His essential and absolute being.

In the book of Hebrews it is written, "Christ said, as he came into the world, 'O God, the blood of bulls and goats cannot satisfy you, so you have made ready this body of mine . . .' He then added, 'Here I am. I have come to give my life.' . . . Under this new plan we have been forgiven and made clean by Christ's dying for us once and for all . . . . And so, dear brothers, now we may walk right into the very Holy of Holies where God is, because of the blood of Jesus. This is the fresh, new, life-giving way which Christ has opened up for us by tearing the curtain—his human body—to let us into the holy presence of God" (*Hebrews 10:5, 9, 10, 19, 20, The Living Bible*).

9 FEBRUARY

"I glorified Thee on the earth, having accomplished the work which Thou hast given Me to do" (*John 17:4*).

Jesus Christ came into the stream of human history "to seek and to save that which was lost" (*Luke 19:10*). To do this, He had to accomplish all the righteous requirements of a holy, just Father. He did this in thought, word, and deed. Though tempted in all things as we are, yet He was without sin (*Hebrews 4:15*). He once said, "My food is to do the will of Him who sent Me, and to accomplish His work" (*John 4:34*).

In this way Jesus Christ glorified His Father on the earth. It is in this way that Jesus explained the Father to men who had not and could not see God. Jesus is "the image of the invisible God" (*Colossians 1:15*).

"Image . . . implies an archetype of which it is a copy . . . Our Lord said, 'He that hath seen Me hath seen the Father' (*John 14:9*). That is, the Son is the exact reproduction of the

Father, a derived image. The other idea involved . . . is that of manifestation, the manifestation of the hidden . . . (Jesus Christ) is the revelation of the Unseen Father, whether pre-incarnate or incarnate."[4] If you want to know what God is like, take a long look at the Lord Jesus Christ.

4. Kenneth Wuest, Word Studies in the Greek New Testament, Book 10, Ephesians and Colossians (Grand Rapids: Eerdmans, © 1953), pp. 182, 183. Used by permission.

10 FEBRUARY

"But when He, the Spirit of truth, comes . . .
He shall glorify Me; for He shall take of Mine,
and shall disclose it to you" (John 16:13, 14).

God sent forth His Son to make Himself known to man. The Son, in fulfilling His assignment, glorified the Father. When Jesus Christ's earthly mission was fulfilled He said, "I will ask the Father, and He will give you another Helper, that He may be with you forever; that is the Spirit of truth" (*John 14:16, 17*).

It is the Holy Spirit's function to make Jesus Christ known to men. As He fulfills this, His mission, He glorifies Jesus Christ. He will never focus on Himself or His work to a degree that obliterates one's view and experience of Jesus Christ. "He will guide you into *all* the truth" (*John 16:13*). To do this, He must guide you into truth about Himself and His work. But if you learn something about Him, it is designed to lead you into a deeper relationship with Jesus Christ. The end result of His work in you is always to clarify your experiential knowledge of Jesus Christ and to be conformed into His likeness. When that happens, not only is Jesus Christ glorified, the Father is glorified as well.

11 FEBRUARY

"But when He, the Spirit of truth, comes, He will guide you into all the truth; for He will not speak on His own initiative, but whatever He hears, He will speak; and He will disclose to you what is to come" (*John 16:13*).

It is interesting to note that when Jesus Christ became man and served His Father humbly here on earth, He indicated the origin of His teaching to be the Father (*John 7:16*). When Jesus Christ went back into heaven to be with His Father, they sent the Holy Spirit into the world to carry on the work Jesus Christ began.

As the Holy Spirit carried out His task, He did not do it on His own initiative. He spoke what He heard. Jesus Christ said of Him, "He shall glorify Me; for He shall take of Mine, and shall disclose it to you" (*John 16:14*). Earlier Jesus Christ had said, "But the Helper, the Holy Spirit, whom the Father will send in My name, He will teach you all things, and bring to your remembrance all that I said to you" (*John 14:26*).

It is the Holy Spirit who inspired the apostles and their associates to write the books of the New Testament in direct fulfillment of Jesus Christ's words. Though the books were written years after the death of Christ (John's Gospel about sixty years after the death of Christ), the very words of Jesus Christ were remembered. Besides this, the Holy Spirit gave understanding so that Christ's words were properly interpreted and explained. Praise God for this work of the Holy Spirit.

12 FEBRUARY

"For to us God revealed them through the Spirit; for the Spirit searches all things, even the depths of God. For who among men knows the thoughts of

*a man except the spirit of the man, which is in him? Even
so the thoughts of God no one knows except the Spirit of
God. Now we have received, not the spirit of the world, but
the Spirit who is from God, that we might know the things
freely given to us by God" (1 Corinthians 2:10-12).*

The word "revealed" expresses the Greek word meaning
"to uncover, to lay open what has been veiled or covered
up." The Holy Spirit who knew fully what had been covered in ages past uncovered that truth about God to "us"—
Paul and the other writers of Scripture.

If you were to meet a total stranger you would gain an
impression of the kind of person he is by what you saw:
height, size, color, clothing, etc. But what that person was
in his innermost being would be inscrutable to you. Only
that person knows what is in his innermost heart. Unless, of
course, he began sharing his heart with you.

Apply that to God and you have the same truth to an
infinitely greater degree. There are some things that can be
known of God by what is seen in the world He created. But
His innermost heart remains a secret unless He reveals
Himself to man. Only the Holy Spirit knows the innermost
secrets of God's nature and truth; therefore He alone is
capable of sharing, revealing, uncovering the things in the
heart of God to the Gospel writers.

13 FEBRUARY

*"For to us God revealed them . . . which things
we also speak, not in words taught by human
wisdom, but in those taught by the Spirit, combining spiritual thoughts with spiritual words" (1 Corinthians 2:10, 13).*

Having revealed truth which had been concealed for ages,
the Holy Spirit then proceeds to inspire the recipients of
revelation to communicate that revelation clearly and
correctly. He does not do so by merely dictating what is to
be said, making the writers mere secretaries. No, He oversees

their writing so that the correct words out of the writers'
vocabulary are chosen to most correctly express the truth.
This goes far beyond human ingenuity. Man at best would
be incapable of making such selections accurately *all the
time*.

Led by the Holy Spirit, the writers meditated on the truth
revealed and compared the words at their disposal with that
truth. They rejected the words and combinations of words
that the Holy Spirit indicated would not correctly express
the truth. Through that process they finally came upon the
words and combinations of words that the Holy Spirit
approved. Thus they expressed their own personalities,
education, and style while being guided to produce a
verbally infallible record of what God wanted said.

14 FEBRUARY

*"But a natural man does not accept the things
of the Spirit of God; for they are foolishness to
him, and he cannot understand them, because they are
spiritually appraised. But he who is spiritual appraises all
things, yet he himself is appraised by no man"*
(*1 Corinthians 2:14, 15*).

After discussing "revelation" and "inspiration," Paul
explains "illumination." This is the process by which God
helps the believer understand what was revealed and
recorded. This process does not take place in the life of one
who has not been born again, the natural man. Such do not
have the Holy Spirit residing in them to be their teacher. To
them what God has revealed is mere foolishness.

Even if they tried, natural men can't understand the
things of God because they must be spiritually discerned.
"The Greek word translated 'discern' means 'to investigate,
inquire into, scrutinize, sift, question.' Thus the
investigation of, inquiry into, scrutinizing, and sifting of
Scripture truth is done in the energy of the Holy Spirit who

illuminates the sacred page of Scripture to the believer. It is 'he that is spiritual' that judgeth all things. The word 'judgeth' is the translation of the same Greek word rendered 'discerneth.' The Spirit-controlled Christian investigates, inquires into, and scrutinizes the Bible and comes to an appreciation and understanding of its contents."[5]

5. Kenneth Wuest, Word Studies in the Greek New Testament, Book 15, In These Last Days (Grand Rapids: Eerdmans, © 1954), p. 43. Used by permission.

15 FEBRUARY

"Being darkened in their understanding, excluded from the life of God, because of the ignorance that is in them, because of the hardness of their heart" (Ephesians 4:18).

Man was created in God's image with a moral and rational ability to fellowship with Him. When, as an act of his own free will, he chose to disobey God, his understanding became darkened. We are all children of darkness. As one prophet said, "All of us like sheep have gone astray, each of us has turned to his own way" (Isaiah 53:6).

Darkness and ignorance go hand in hand. Ignorance of one's surroundings in a strange, dark room is dispelled when you turn on some light. Man, through disobedience, has hardened his heart against God and His revealed will. He has rejected the light which God has given him. Therefore, he is left to grope in the darkness of spiritual ignorance. In that condition he is excluded from the life of God.

It is with this truth about the present condition of men outside of salvation through Jesus Christ that John wrote, "And this is the message we have heard from Him and announce to you, that God is light, and in Him there is no darkness at all. If we say that we have fellowship with Him and yet walk in the darkness, we lie and do not practice the truth" (*1 John 1:5, 6*).

16 FEBRUARY

ALL WE NEED—DEUTERONOMY (twelve days to read)

"The Lord your God has watched over you and blessed you every step of the way for all these forty years as you have wandered around in this great wilderness; and you have lacked nothing in all that time" (Deuteronomy 2:7, The Living Bible).

Have you ever heard it said, "Where God guides He provides"? Is this true?

As you read Deuteronomy, notice that throughout Israel's wilderness wanderings God provided for them so that they lacked nothing. He gave them spiritual support through His law, moral support by repeating His promise to give them Canaan, protection by pledging His own presence and power, and guidance through Moses and Joshua. God's provisions were abundant and all-embracing.

His provisions are determined by our needs. Our needs are determined by our physical, social, and spiritual circumstances. And these, in turn, are determined by our obedience to God's guidance. Yes, and even when we at times are unfaithful, He remains faithful. Therefore, it's true: where God guides He provides.

17 FEBRUARY

"If our gospel be hid, it is hid to them that are lost" (2 Corinthians 4:3, KJV).

The Bible reveals man as hopelessly lost. The vast

majority of people don't want to face this fact about themselves, but if we honestly look at the facts we must agree with God's revealed conclusion. Both in the Bible and in recorded history those who were closest to God saw themselves as the vilest of sinners. Note Isaiah's, Job's, and the Psalmist's view of themselves and of men around them when they were experiencing a face to face encounter with God.

If you are quite self-assured and positive about human nature, this is not a sign you are living close to God. It is more a sign of your estrangement from God's presence. Be careful lest you put yourself in the category of those Jesus Christ identified as thinking themselves well and not needing a physician. Christ came "to seek and to save that which was lost" (*Luke 19:10*). He will respond to you and meet your need if, and only if, you acknowledge your need to Him.

18 FEBRUARY

"And you were dead in your trespasses and sins" (*Ephesians 2:1*).

Man as a sinner is not characterized only by darkness and ignorance. He is also said to be dead. God told Adam not to eat of a certain fruit tree in the garden of Eden, for in the day he would eat of it he would surely die (*Genesis 2:16, 17*). When Adam ate of that tree he did not die physically right away. However, he did experience an alienation from God. Sin came between him and God. Such separation is spiritual death.

James refers to the deadliness of sin when he writes, "Each one is tempted when he is carried away and enticed by his own lust. Then when lust has conceived, it gives birth to sin; and when sin is accomplished, it brings forth death" (*James 1:14, 15*). Paul puts it succinctly: "The wages of sin is death" (*Romans 6:23*).

But the Psalmist declares, "I was brought forth in iniquity, and in sin my mother conceived me" (*Psalm 51:5*). If spiritual death is related to sin, then since we are born in sin, we are born spiritually dead. This is why it is important to understand that Jesus Christ was miraculously conceived and thus free from the sinful nature we all inherit. In Him no sin could be found.

We are not sinners because we have committed sins. We commit sins because we are sinners. "The Lord looks down from heaven on all mankind to see if there are any who are wise, who want to please God. But no, all have strayed away; all are rotten with sin. Not one is good, not one!" (*Psalm 14:2, 3, The Living Bible*).

19 FEBRUARY

"By this the children of God and the children of the devil are obvious" (*1 John 3:10*).

No such teaching as the universal Fatherhood of God appears in the Bible. He did create all men and therefore it is legitimate to conclude that they are His offspring (*Acts 17:28*). And man does exist in God's presence. But it is only through faith in Jesus Christ that we become His "sons," His "children."

"But if you keep on sinning, it shows that you belong to Satan, who since he first began to sin has kept steadily at it. But the Son of God came to destroy these works of the devil. The person who has been born into God's family does not make a practice of sinning, because God's new life is in him; so he can't keep on sinning, for this new life has been born into him and controls him—he has been born again" (*1 John 3:8, 9, The Living Bible*). Paul reminds all who are children of God: "You formerly walked according to the course of this world, according to the prince of the power of the air, of the spirit that is now working in the sons of disobedience" (*Ephesians 2:2*).

It is not popular to consider those who do not believe in Jesus Christ as children of the devil. Jesus Christ, however, did just that. He said, "If God were your Father, you would love Me; for I proceeded forth and have come from God, for I have not even come on My own initiative, but He sent Me. Why do you not understand what I am saying? It is because you cannot hear My word. You are of your father the devil" (*John 8:42-44*).

20 FEBRUARY

"You are of your father the devil, and you want to do the desires of your father. He was a murderer from the beginning, and does not stand in the truth, because there is no truth in him. Whenever he speaks a lie, he speaks from his own nature; for he is a liar, and the father of lies" (John 8:44).

Jesus Christ said, "I am the truth" (*John 14:6*). Truth finds its source in God. God is the Father of truth. The archenemy of God, the devil, is the father of lies. It is as much his nature to tell lies as it is for Jesus Christ to tell the truth. Lies, deception, slander, evil speaking, gossip, malice, quarrelsomeness, agitation, rioting, murder, wars, etc. all find their ultimate source in the devil.

Whenever you wonder about the atrocities which have occurred in the records of human history—how could anyone do such things?—remember the nature of the devil. He finds fiendish delight in seeing those created in God's image suffering agony. He wants you to think that God is to blame for your suffering. He wants you to curse God, to turn from God. He does his utmost to deceive you into thinking that God is really not interested in your well-being. Remember Job? Even his counselors had a tendency to blame Job and/or God. The real culprit, however, was the devil, Satan. He goes about as a roaring lion seeking whom he may devour (*1 Peter 5:8*).

21 FEBRUARY

"The prince of the power of the air"
(Ephesians 2:2).

When the devil, also referred to as Satan, rebelled against God, he was judged and relegated to a certain realm. Paul describes his present position in the reference quoted above.

The Greek word for *prince* refers to the first in an order of persons or things. Here it refers to Satan, who is the first one in power and authority within his kingdom. The word *power* refers to demons. The word *air* no doubt refers to the lower atmosphere where we human beings are. Satan and his demon hordes, burning with intense hatred toward God and His unique plan for man, prey upon the human race, seeking to thwart God's good purposes. The unsaved are in his grip. They follow his dictates in their behavior.

Satan's influence is growing and manifesting itself especially in the realm of false religions whose origins Paul ascribes to demons. "But the Spirit explicitly says that in later times some will fall away from the faith, paying attention to deceitful spirits and doctrines of demons" *(1 Timothy 4:1).*

22 FEBRUARY

"The Son of God appeared for this purpose, that He might destroy the works of the devil"
(1 John 3:8).

The works of the devil are designed to lead us into disobedience to the will of God. He wants to frustrate the purpose of God for His creation, especially His purpose for man. After man sinned in the Garden of Eden, God pronounced a judgment upon the serpent, the devil: "I will put enmity between you and the woman, and between your seed and her seed; He shall bruise you on the head, and you shall bruise him on the heel" *(Genesis 3:15).* From the time of Adam until the time of Christ, Satan tried to overcome that judgment, but he never succeeded more than to bruise the heel of the seed of the woman. (Consider *Genesis 4, Esther, Matthew 2*.)

In the earthly lifetime of Jesus Christ, there were many attempts made to thwart the will of God in His life. The struggle intensified as His earthly ministry drew to a close. Satan was sure that if he could snuff out the life of Jesus Christ, he would win the struggle. But he was ignorant of the plan of God fulfilled on the cross.

"Our words are wise because they are from God . . . the great men of the world would have not understood it; if they had, they never would have crucified the Lord of glory" (*1 Corinthians 2:7, 8, The Living Bible*). "He thus stripped the principalities and dominions of power and made a public display of them, triumphing over them by the cross" (*Colossians 2:15, Williams*).

23 FEBRUARY

"For the word of the cross is to those who are perishing foolishness, but to us who are being saved it is the power of God" (1 Corinthians 1:18).

Satan was ignorant of God's eternal plan through the cross. The rulers of Jesus Christ's day were ignorant of the significance of the cross also. Today there are still millions who think of the cross of Jesus Christ as insignificant. To them it is mere foolishness to believe that what happened on the cross almost 2,000 years ago has any potential effect on someone today.

But to the one whose eyes have been opened to the truth of God, the cross is the power of God. It was God's way of releasing the stranglehold Satan had on the human race. It was God's way of shattering the shackles of sin gripping every man. It was God's way of demonstrating His love toward us while we were yet in our sin (*Romans 5:8*). Over and over the word of the cross re-echoes throughout the Word of God. It is the basis for our hope. It is the foundation of our reconciliation to God. It rightfully should be our only boast: "God forbid that I should boast about anything except the cross of our Lord Jesus Christ" (*Galatians 6:14, The Living Bible*).

24 FEBRUARY

"He made Him who knew no sin to be sin on our behalf, that we might become the righteousness of God in Him" (*2 Corinthians 5:21*).

This verse is the New Testament equivalent of Isaiah 53:5, 6: "He was pierced through for our transgressions, He was crushed for our iniquities; the chastening for our well-being fell upon Him, and by His scourging we are healed. All of us like sheep have gone astray, each of us has turned to his own way; but the Lord has caused the iniquity of us all to fall on Him."

"We were sick unto death because of our sins; but He, the sinless one, took upon Himself a suffering unto death, which was, as it were, the concentration and essence of the woes that we had deserved; and this voluntary endurance, this submission to the justice of the Holy One, in accordance with the counsels of divine love, became the source of our healing."[6]

When on the cross, Jesus Christ cried out, "My God, My God, why hast Thou forsaken Me?" (*Matthew 27:46*). This is a mystery. How could God the Father forsake God the Son? Commentator Delitzsch suggests an answer in his discussion of Isaiah 53:6: "What other reason could there be for God's not rescuing Him from this the bitterest cup of death, than the ethical impossibility of acknowledging the atonement as really made, without having left the representative of the guilty, who had presented Himself to

Him as though guilty Himself, to taste of the punishment
which they had deserved?"[7]

6. Op. cit. Vol. 7, Keil and Delitzsch, pp.
319, 320.
7. Ibid., p. 321.

25 FEBRUARY

"He is also head of the body, the church"
(Colossians 1:18).

One of the clearest designations for the Church of Jesus
Christ is *the body of Christ*. Christ is the head of His body,
the Church. We become members of His body when we
become Christians through faith in Jesus Christ. Paul
describes this process as follows: "Our bodies have many
parts, but the many parts make up only one body when
they are all put together. So it is with the 'body' of Christ.
Each of us is a part of the one body of Christ. Some of us
are Jews, some are Gentiles, some are slaves and some are
free. But the Holy Spirit has fitted us all together into one
body. We have been baptized into Christ's body by the one
Spirit, and have all been given that same Holy Spirit. Yes,
the body has many parts" (*1 Corinthians 12:12-14, The
Living Bible*). The baptizing work of the Spirit is done when
He places us into our unique position in the body of Christ.

Once we are in the body of Christ, we have a specific
function to fulfill. The Spirit equips us for that specific
function by giving us one or more spiritual gifts
(*1 Corinthians 12*). We should seek to discover, understand
and use the gift(s) of the Spirit given to us. Only when each
member of the body of Christ does his task faithfully will
Christ be able to fulfill His objective through His body.

26 FEBRUARY

"And He gave some as apostles, and some as prophets, and some as evangelists, and some as pastors and teachers" (Ephesians 4:11).

Not only does each member of the body of Christ have a gift or gifts for fulfilling his specific task; Christ sees to it that gifted men are given to the Church for enrichment and encouragement.

Specifically they are given to the Church for the perfecting or equipping of the saints for the work of the ministry—for the edifying or "building up of the body of Christ; until we all attain to the unity of the faith, and of the knowledge of the Son of God, to a mature man, to the measure of the stature which belongs to the fulness of Christ. As a result, we are no longer to be children, tossed here and there by waves, and carried about by every wind of doctrine, by the trickery of men, by craftiness in deceitful scheming" (*Ephesians 4:12-14*). Gifted leaders are given to the Church to help the saints discover their gifts and to guide and encourage them in the use of their gifts. The full picture is that every one in the Church helps each other in the growing, maturing process.

The gifted leaders are not to do all the work and ministry in a church. They are to motivate, encourage, oversee and direct a working force which includes everyone in the church.

27 FEBRUARY

"But earnestly desire the greater gifts. And I show you a still more excellent way"
(*1 Corinthians 12:31*).

We should seek to be as useful as possible in furthering the work of God. In that respect, members of the Church are to seek the greater or best gifts. Considering the order in which they are listed in Romans 12 and 1 Corinthians 12 will help in determining which gifts are to be sought. First Corinthians 14 also explains guidelines for such determination. But more important than having all the gifts is what Paul describes as the more excellent way, the way of love.

"If I had the gift of being able to speak in other languages without learning them, and could speak in every language there is in all of heaven and earth, but didn't love others, I would only be making noise. If I had the gift of prophecy and knew all about what is going to happen in the future, knew everything about everything, but didn't love others, what good would it do? Even if I had the gift of faith so that I could speak to a mountain and make it move, I would still be worth nothing at all without love. If I gave everything I have to poor people, and if I were burned alive for preaching the Gospel but didn't love others, it would be of no value whatever.

"Love is very patient and kind, never jealous or envious, never boastful or proud, never haughty or selfish or rude. Love does not demand its own way. It is not irritable or touchy. It does not hold grudges and will hardly even notice when others do it wrong. It is never glad about injustice, but rejoices whenever truth wins out. If you love someone you will be loyal to him no matter what the cost. You will always believe in him, always expect the best of him, and always stand your ground in defending him . . . . Love goes on forever" (*1 Corinthians 13:1-8, The Living Bible*).

28 FEBRUARY

GETTING WHAT GOD GIVES—JOSHUA
(seven days to read)

"This book of the law shall not depart from your mouth, but you shall meditate on it day and night, so that you may be careful to do according to all that is written in it; for

then you will make your way prosperous, and then you will have success" (Joshua 1:8).

The Bible contains thousands of promises God has made to man. Each promise is a gift to receive.

How? In Joshua you will find first that God demands faith expressed in explicit obedience, even when His instructions seem odd, as at Jericho. God also demands sinless obedience. Achan reminds us that all sin must be dealt with before we can possess God's promises. Finally God demands selfless and slackless obedience (*Joshua 18:3*). Never stop short of fully possessing the promise or it will elude you. Learn the promises God has made to you in the Bible. Then trust Him to fulfill them in you as you wholeheartedly obey Him.

1 MARCH

"Do I not fill the heavens and the earth?"
(Jeremiah 23:24).

We are creatures of time and space. God is not confined to either. We have already seen that He is eternal. Now we are confronted with His *omnipresence.* He is everywhere present in the heavens and the earth.

In a unique sense God is present in heaven, which we think of as "way up there." Often when we think of God's greatness, we automatically think of His being far away. But He is also "a God who is near" *(Jeremiah 23:23).* This can be terrifying if you want to hide from Him. Where can you go to hide? He fills every available space. Paul said that God created men "that they should seek after God, and perhaps feel their way toward him and find him—though he is not far from any one of us. For in him we live and move and are" *(Acts 17:27, 28, The Living Bible).*

This truth can be gloriously comforting to the one who by faith hides *in* Him rather than tries to hide *from* Him. We are never orphaned by God. He is always present. You do not have to face any experience alone. "If God is for us, who is against us?" *(Romans 8:31).* With this in mind, the Psalmist bursts forth in praise; "I love Thee, O Lord, my strength. The Lord is my rock and my fortress and my deliverer, My God, my rock, in whom I take refuge" *(Psalm 18:1, 2).*

2 MARCH

"But will God indeed dwell with mankind on the earth? Behold, heaven and the highest heaven cannot contain Thee; how much less this house which I have built. Yet have regard to the prayer of Thy servant and to his supplication . . . hear Thou from Thy dwelling-place, from heaven" (2 Chronicles 6:18-21).

Solomon had built a temple for God, but he was wise enough to recognize that God was too great to be contained in a building built by men. Even all that God had created in all of its vast expanse could not contain God. There are places, however, where God's presence is more manifest than others. Solomon designates such a place, which he refers to as God's dwelling-place, heaven.

Following Solomon's prayer to God, God responded by filling the temple with His glorious presence. So magnificent was His glory that the priests were unable to enter into the house of God (*2 Chronicles 7:2*). Though God is everywhere present, He displays His presence in a unique way in heaven as well as at various places from time to time as He deems wise.

We often invoke God to be present in church gatherings as well as on other occasions. It would be more proper for us to ask God to make us *aware of* and *respectful of* His presence.

3 MARCH

"I will never desert you, nor will I ever forsake you" (*Hebrews 13:5*).

Only God could make a statement like that. This statement is personal and can be appropriated by any true believer. What a comfort to know that I am never alone, nor will I ever be left alone, forsaken. I can say with confidence, "The Lord is my helper, I will not be afraid. What shall man do to me?" (*Hebrews 13:6*).

The only way in which God could fulfill this promise is for God to be omnipresent. Picture seven Christians together. All can rejoice in the knowledge that God is present with them. Now picture six of them traveling away—one to South America, one to North America, one to Europe, one to Africa, one to Asia and one to Australia. When all have arrived at their scattered destinations, each can still enjoy the presence of God just as much as when all were together. If the seventh were to travel to the moon, he could also enjoy the presence of God there. Though separated by these vast distances, each at the very same moment can enjoy the presence of God. Praise God! He is accessible at all times in all places by anyone who seeks after Him.

Prayer takes hold of this truth. Prayer is simply saying, "God, *You are here*. You see my situation. You know my need. Please meet it." Or, "God, *You are with my friend* in need. You see his circumstances. Please help him." Or even, "God, I don't know where my child or friend is. *You*, however, *are with him*. You know his need. Please minister to him." Yes, God is present wherever and whenever needed. And He wants to be recognized and worshiped even when consciously not needed.

4 MARCH

"Behold, I stand at the door and knock; if any one hears My voice and opens the door, I will come in to him" (Revelation 3:20).

The most personal aspect of the truth that Jesus Christ is present everywhere is this promise that He will come into your life as He has entered the lives of millions for almost 2,000 years, if you invite Him into your life by faith.

It is to be noted that the Savior not only knocks but also lifts His voice in calling us to let Him into the deepest recesses of our hearts.

Some years ago King George V and Queen Mary, while vacationing by the seaside, took a walk along the ocean front. When the queen sprained her ankle, the couple was forced to find their way to a nearby cottage to seek assistance. In answer to their knock at the door, a voice called out, "Who's there?" The reply was, "King George and Queen Mary."

"You don't expect me to believe that, do you?" exclaimed the occupant.

"See for yourself," said the king.

Opening the door, the man and his wife immediately invited the royal couple into their home and gave them all the help and hospitality they could. For years they retold the story and always concluded by saying, "You know, we almost refused to let them in!"

The King of Heaven is standing at your heart's door. Will you let Him in? Then you will be able to say, "Christ in me, the hope of glory" (*Colossians 1:27*).

5 MARCH

"Lo, I am with you always" (*Matthew 28:20*).

This is Jesus Christ speaking. He had just finished challenging His disciples with the great commission: "Go therefore and make disciples of all nations, baptizing them in the name of the Father and the Son and the Holy Spirit, teaching them to observe all that I commanded you" (*Matthew 28:19, 20*). He was anticipating His disciples going out to the distant corners of the world proclaiming the Good News, establishing disciples and churches. And in the light of that anticipated global outreach, He was making a promise: "I am with you always, even to the end of the age." Jesus never asked His servants to go anywhere without the guarantee that He would be there with them.

To fulfill His promise, Jesus Christ would have to be omnipresent. To be omnipresent He would have to be God. If He were not God, His promise would involve a gross deception and would undermine the whole thrust of the gospel.

Christ implied His omnipresence also in a statement in John 3:13, KJV: "And no man hath ascended up to heaven, but he that came down from heaven, even the Son of man which is in heaven." At the very moment when He was referring to the Son of man being in heaven, He, the Son of man, was bodily present with them on earth.

6 MARCH

"For where two or three have gathered together in My name, there I am in their midst" (*Matthew 18:20*).

Here is another promise made possible only because Jesus Christ is omnipresent. He was in the flesh when He made this promise, and obviously He couldn't be bodily present wherever two or three gather in His name. Now He is at His Father's right hand in His resurrection body. But wherever the above conditions are met, He is faithful in fulfilling His promise: "I am in their midst."

So many of us need supplemental elements to aid us in worship. Just viewing the beauty of a nature scene evokes in many a sense of worship. Beautiful architectural structures, often created at great expense, seem necessary for some to get into a worshipful attitude. For others, a well-prepared program of song and word is indispensable. The promise of Christ's presence, however, is all that is necessary. Strip away all the other parts of our worship experiences, but as long as you have Jesus Christ present you have all that you need.

7 MARCH

POLLUTING OUR POSSESSIONS—JUDGES
(six days to read)
"And it came about when Israel became strong, that they

put the Canaanites to forced labor, but they did not drive them out completely" (Judges 1:28).

Never trifle with God or what He has given you. You will always lose out if you do. Partial or periodic obedience such as you will see throughout Judges just isn't good enough.

Samson, the colorful judge, illustrates this principle which is so common. He played around with what God had given him until he lost it. And his loss affected all the people whom he judged. Only repentance and faith saved his life from total loss.

Our possessions, no matter how precious they might be to us now, will become worthless to us and others if we sinfully and selfishly trifle with them.

8 MARCH

"Where can I go from Thy Spirit? Or where can I flee from Thy presence?" (Psalm 139:7).

The Psalmist begins this Psalm with the declaration that God knows him through and through. The implication he leaves you with is that he is ashamed to stand before God who knows what he is like. He would sooner flee and hide from God. But where could he go to hide? Really, where *could* he go?

He confesses, "If I go up to heaven, you are there; if I go down to the place of the dead, you are there. If I ride the morning winds to the farthest oceans, even there your hand will guide me, your strength will support me"
(*Psalm 139:8-10, The Living Bible*).

Only the fool tries to run from God. It is futile to try to get away from Him. It is fulfilling to run *to* God. The focus in this portion is on God the Holy Spirit. He, together with the Father and the Son, is omnipresent. He is referred to in the Bible as the eyes of the Lord (*Revelation 5:6*). The words of Hanani to Asa are still true: "The eyes of the Lord move to and fro throughout the earth that He may strongly support those whose heart is completely His" (*2 Chronicles 16:9;* compare *Zechariah 4*). God the Holy Spirit is ever present to bless you if you are "blessable."

9 MARCH

"I will ask the Father, and He will give you another Helper, that He may be with you forever; that is the Spirit of truth, . . . you know Him because He abides with you, and will be in you" (John 14:16-17).

Jesus comforts His disciples with the promise that He will never leave them as orphans (*John 14:18*). He will ask His Father to give them another Helper. The word "another" refers to another of the same kind. The Holy Spirit is the same kind of Helper as Jesus Christ was to His disciples. The only difference is that though Jesus Christ had to leave them bodily and return to His Father in Heaven, the Holy Spirit, not being limited by a body, could and would remain within each true believer wherever he or she might go. That which distinctively identifies one as being a Christian is the Holy Spirit's indwelling (*Romans 8:9*).

The Holy Spirit dwells within the Church of Jesus Christ (*1 Corinthians 3:16*). When the members of the Church disperse and go out into the world, wherever they go it is still true that the Holy Spirit indwells the Church because He indwells every member individually. This is hard for us to grasp intellectually. Even more difficult to understand is the promise of Jesus Christ that if we are obedient to His Word as an expression of our love to Him, His Father will love us and the Father and the Son will come to dwell in us (*John 14:23*). Amazing as it might seem, we can enjoy the presence and fellowship of our triune God in our day to day world.

10 MARCH

"The soul who sins will die" (Ezekiel 18:4).
Man, born in sin and practicing sin, is
spiritually dead, separated from God, even while being alive
physically. If he continues in that state, he will experience
not only physical death as appointed, but also judgment
(*Hebrews 9:27*). Jesus once challenged unbelievers, "You
will die in your sins; for unless you believe that I am the
Messiah, the Son of God, you will die in your sins" (*John
8:24, The Living Bible*). What this means was explained
further by Jesus when He said, "Don't be so surprised!
Indeed the time is coming when all the dead in their graves
shall hear the voice of God's Son, and shall rise again . . .
those who have continued in evil, to judgment" (*John 5:28,
29, The Living Bible*).

In that judgment the unbelieving will stand before God to
hear the verdict: "And I saw a great white throne and Him
who sat upon it, from whose presence earth and heaven fled
away, and no place was found for them. And I saw the
dead, the great and the small, standing before the throne,
and books were opened; and another book was opened,
which is the book of life; and the dead were judged from the
things which were written in the books, according to their
deeds. And the sea gave up the dead which were in it, and
death and Hades gave up the dead which were in them; and
they were judged, every one of them according to their
deeds. And death and Hades were thrown into the lake of
fire. This is the second death, the lake of fire" (*Revelation
20:11-14*).

11 MARCH

*"They were judged, every one of them
according to their deeds" (Revelation 20:13).*
Man goes to hell and experiences the second death only
because he rejects God's provision and offer of salvation. As

a part of that judgment, however, an evaluation is made of all that he did in his earthly life. God is not a respecter of persons. He weighs all the facts about an individual's life. Only then does He declare the details of his judgment.

There is reason to believe that in hell there will be degrees of punishment. Jesus Christ did many wonderful works in the cities of Chorazin, Bethsaida and Capernaum. The response of the people, however, was cold and indifferent. This prompted Jesus to say, "Woe to you . . . . For if the miracles I did in your streets had been done in wicked Tyre and Sidon their people would have repented long ago in shame and humility. Truly, Tyre and Sidon will be better off on the Judgment Day than you" (*Matthew 11:21, 22, The Living Bible*).

To whom much has been given, of him God will require much. Those who die in their sins in heathen darkness, ignorant of the good news in Christ, will be eternally separated from God, but the degree of their punishment will be less than those who die in their sins having known about the message of forgiveness through Christ. Woe to those who die in their sins after living in a spiritually enlightened atmosphere!

12 MARCH

"Enemies of the cross of Christ, whose end is destruction" (Philippians 3:18, 19).

The Bible teaches that everyone who does not know the Lord Jesus Christ at the time of his death "will be punished in everlasting hell, forever separated from the Lord, never to see the glory of his power" (*2 Thessalonians 1:9, The Living Bible*). There is no possibility of being transferred from that state of being separated from God. Never will they have the opportunity of hoping for even the slightest degree of mercy. They will be doomed for eternity. When Paul spoke of this, tears came into his eyes (*Philippians 3:18*).

Dr. R. A. Torrey, a great evangelist of the nineteenth century, came to the following searching conclusion: "If you really believe the doctrine of the endless, conscious torment of the impenitent, and the doctrine really gets hold of you, you will work as you never worked before for the salvation of the lost. If you in any wise abate the doctrine, it will abate your zeal. Time and again the author has come up to this awful doctrine and tried to find some way of escape from it, but when he has failed, as he always has at last, when he was honest with the Bible and with himself, he has returned to his work with an increased burden for souls and an intensified determination to spend and be spent for their salvation."[8]

8. *R. A. Torrey, What the Bible Teaches (Old Tappan, N. J.: Revell, © 1933), p. 313. Used by permission.*

13 MARCH

PRIZING WHAT WE HAVE—RUTH (one day to read)

"But Ruth said, 'Do not urge me to leave you or turn back from following you; for where you go, I will go, and where you lodge, I will lodge. Your people shall be my people, and your God, my God' " (Ruth 1:16).

"Little is much when God is in it," wrote A. A. Rees.

Through marriage Ruth discovered the God of Israel. When her husband died she determined not to lose her new faith, whatever the cost. When she left family, friends, and home to live with widowed Naomi, her experience was hard. But humbly and obediently she held on. And God blessed her for it. As a foreigner she married into the family through which Jesus Christ was born into the world.

Ruth seemed to have little to start with, but by prizing what she had, she saw it multiplied. We too will find true prosperity only when we follow the simple principle of prizing and utilizing what we already have from the hand of God.

14 MARCH

HONOR THROUGH HUMILITY—
1 SAMUEL (ten days to read)

"But the Lord said to Samuel, 'Do not look at his appearance or at the height of his stature, because I have rejected him; for God sees not as man sees, for man looks at the outward appearance, but the Lord looks at the heart'" (1 Samuel 16:7).

"Just as water ever seeks and fills the lowest place, so the moment God finds you abased and empty, His glory and power flow in" (Andrew Murray). Jesus said, "Those who humble themselves shall be exalted" *(Matthew 23:12, The Living Bible)*. This principle has always operated in God's dealings with man.

Samuel, Saul, and David were all exalted to places of importance because of their initial humility. The moment Saul became proud and selfish, he robbed himself of God's blessing and David was anointed to replace him as king of Israel.

. Much can be learned from the lives of these three men. But the practical principle—"God gives special blessings to those who are humble, but sets himself against those who are proud" *(1 Peter 5:5, The Living Bible)*—is the most important. Learn it well!

15 MARCH

*"And if anyone's name was not found written
in the book of life, he was thrown into the lake
of fire" (Revelation 20:15).*

There is only one way for man to escape the inevitable
great white throne judgment: have his name written in the
Lamb's book of life. If it isn't, he will be cast into the lake
of fire, which is the second death.

Note here that God did not make hell for man. God did
not plan to send man there. God made hell for the devil and
his angels *(Matthew 25:41)*. If man, however, refuses to
prepare himself for the eternal state God desires for all men
(1 Timothy 2:4; 2 Peter 3:9), then he essentially sends
himself to hell. God complies with man's wish to go where
his own selfish will directs him.

How do you get your name written into the Lamb's book
of life? You must become the Lamb's possession. He puts
the names of all those who belong to Him into His book of
life. He died on the cross to purchase your deliverance and
gain your possession. If you recognize that fact, accept it to
be true for you, and turn your life over to Jesus Christ by
faith, your name will be put into the Lamb's book of life.
Then you are secure for time and eternity. "So there is now
no condemnation awaiting those who belong to Christ
Jesus" *(Romans 8:1, The Living Bible)*.

16 MARCH

*"God has not destined us for wrath, but for
obtaining salvation through our Lord Jesus
Christ" (1 Thessalonians 5:9).*

Some think that once God created the world and its
inhabitants, He left them to their own devices to develop or
deteriorate accordingly. Others believe that God destined
some for hell and some for salvation, purely on an arbitrary

basis. Others believe that God responds to man's initiative. Man chooses his own destiny.

The human mind has a hard time thinking in terms other than black and white. It is therefore difficult to understand that the Bible teaches *both*. God determines those who will obtain salvation, and man chooses with his own free will whether or not he will accept salvation.

It is true that whosoever will may come (*John 3:16*). It is also true, however, that no man can come except God the Father draw him (*John 6:44*). Man can never argue, "I won't decide to trust in Christ because God never chose me." Man is responsible for his decisions. On the other hand, man cannot boast about his decision to trust in Christ because he would not have made that decision had not God drawn him. Praise God for His invitation to you to trust in Him. Praise Him, when you come, that He is drawing you.

17 MARCH

"Whom He foreknew, He also predestined to become conformed to the image of His Son" (*Romans 8:29*).

This is God taking the initiative in a life. In His wisdom He selects an individual and predestines him to become conformed to the image of His Son Jesus Christ. Does God ever fail in this project? Paul answers by describing the process God uses. "Whom He predestined, these He also called: and whom He called, these He also justified; and whom He justified, these He also glorified" (*Romans 8:30*). All of those predestined are ultimately glorified. His call to those He predestines is an effectual call—there is always a positive response. All who thus respond are justified. This is a judicial act of God whereby He declares one to be free from guilt. This does not mean the person is perfect in his conduct while here on earth. It does mean that he is guaranteed ultimate victory in which he is glorified—made like the Lord Jesus Christ.

God, being God, guarantees the success of this process. If He is for us, no one can frustrate His plan (*Romans 8:31-38*).

18 MARCH

"Whoever will call upon the name of the Lord will be saved" (Romans 10:13).

In this invitation, Paul focuses on the human aspect of salvation. Human responsibility is not limited to a moment's response—"whoever will call." It includes the responsibility to proclaim. Note Paul's argument: "But how shall they ask him to save them unless they believe in him? And how can they believe in him if they have never heard about him? And how can they hear about him unless someone tells them? And how will anyone go and tell them unless someone sends him?" (*Romans 10:14, 15, The Living Bible*).

In this line of reasoning, the possibility of anyone coming to Jesus Christ rests upon the faithfulness of God's *people* in spreading the Good News, as well as the willingness of the hearer to respond. If no one goes out to proclaim the good news, the uninformed remain uninformed; and being uninformed they remain in bondage. Only when one comes to know the truth is he set free (*John 8:32*). Whoever knows the truth about God's provision can accept it for himself. When he does he is saved. His response is the key.

19 MARCH

"They are without excuse" (Romans 1:20).

There are those who will argue that God is not righteous if He condemns those who could not respond to the good news because they have never heard it. Millions upon millions are in that condition in our present world. Would a God of love allow this?

In writing about Jesus, John says, "There was the true light which, coming into the world, enlightens every man" (*John 1:9*). In some way, Jesus, who is the light of the world, enlightens every man. Evidently every man has a measure of light concerning truth. Paul argues, "That which is known about God is evident within them; for God made it evident to them. For since the creation of the world His invisible attributes, His eternal power and divine nature, have been clearly seen, being understood through what has been made, so that they are without excuse" (*Romans 1:19, 20.*) He also points out there is evidence that the Law of God is "written in their hearts, their conscience bearing witness, and their thoughts alternately accusing or else defending themselves" (*Romans 2:15*).

In other words, every human being has some light concerning truth. If he follows the light he has received, then God, being loving and righteous, will give him more light. If he continues following the light God gives him, God will ultimately confront him with the light of the world, Jesus Christ. How He does this is His responsibility. *That* He does it is demonstrated in the record concerning the conversion of Cornelius (*Acts 10*).

20 MARCH

"For we wanted to come to you—I, Paul, more than once—and yet Satan thwarted us"
(*1 Thessalonians 2:18*).

The job of getting the good news out to the people demands discipline and sacrifice. Unknown to many, a spiritual warfare is going on all the time, with the forces of darkness fiercely opposing the spreading of the good news.

In the Old Testament we have the account of God's answer to Daniel's prayer being delayed by spiritual forces opposed to the will of God (*Daniel 10:12, 13*). In the New Testament you have many accounts of how Satan and his forces sought to frustrate and resist the advance of God's kingdom. Paul writes of how he made efforts to go to certain places to share the Christian faith, but was hindered from doing so. He didn't give up, though. It was a daily struggle of faith to withstand the wiles of Satan (*Ephesians 6:10-18*). Paul recognized that evil forces were behind human resistance and persecution. This is why he could lovingly go on seeking to reach the lost for Christ. He also recognized he had a responsibility to watch his own life and example while preaching to others (*1 Corinthians 9:27*).

21 MARCH

"Now here is the explanation of the story I told about the farmer planting grain: The hard path where some of the seeds fell represents the heart of a person who hears the Good News about the Kingdom and doesn't understand it; then Satan comes and snatches away the seeds from his heart" (Matthew 13:18, 19, The Living Bible).

Jesus was aware of the work of the evil one, Satan. In discussing the work of spreading the Word of God as a sower spreads seed, Jesus describes Satan's strategy. When the seed falls beside the road, the birds come and pick it up. Jesus interpreted this as the experience of one who has not been prepared by the Spirit. When he hears the Word of God, before it finds lodging in his mind and heart, Satan comes and removes it.

We must be aware of this work of Satan whenever we seek to spread the Word of God. He goes where we go. He seeks to undo all that we endeavor to do for the cause of Christ. This is why follow-up is so crucial; we must reinforce over and over again that which we communicate. Seldom does a nonbeliever respond to the first presentation of the good news. Satan's work hinders him.

It is at least implied that Satan has access to the mind of man. He can influence one's thoughts by the power of suggestion. He will do his utmost to inject thoughts totally contrary to the Word of God when he senses someone is considering following the Lord. Expect this battle for man's mind whenever you engage in spreading the good news, and prepare to be thorough in your work.

22 MARCH

"And the Lord added to the church daily such as should be saved" (Acts 2:47, KJV).

The Lord promised to build His Church. To do this, He gave His Church the great mandate, "Go therefore and make disciples" *(Matthew 28:19)*. He also gave His Church the Holy Spirit to quicken and motivate her for this task *(Acts 1:8)*. He then set up the circumstances which were most conducive for seeing the task fulfilled. Note what took place on Pentecost *(Acts 2)*. As you read the book of Acts, it becomes obvious it is not primarily a record of the acts of the apostles. It is through and through a record of God working through His people.

At times God moved multitudes to respond to the good news: 3,000 *(Acts 2:41)*, 5,000 men *(Acts 4:4)*, citywide *(Acts 8:5-8)*. At other times He worked mightily to reach one or two at a time: a man of Ethiopia *(Acts 8:27)*, Saul, later to become the great apostle Paul *(Acts 9:11)*, Cornelius *(Acts 10)*. Down through the centuries of church history, the Lord has added such as should be saved, sometimes by drawing multitudes into the fold, at other times singling out individuals. Obviously mission and evangelism were essential elements of church life. Church growth was the natural result.

23 MARCH

"Christ Jesus Himself being the cornerstone"
(Ephesians 2:20).

When referring to the Church as His body, Jesus Christ is always presented as its Head. When referring to the Church as a building, Jesus Christ is presented as the foundation or as the cornerstone. You can't build without a cornerstone. If there are a number of cornerstones, then one is selected as the chief cornerstone, the most essential, without which there would not be an adequate starting place from which to proceed building. Jesus Christ is that chief cornerstone. The whole building is fitted together with Him (*Ephesians 2:21*).

Peter refers to Jesus Christ as a "living stone" (*1 Peter 2:4*). The stones which are fitted together with Him to make up a spiritual house also are referred to as living stones (*1 Peter 2:5*). The Church is not brick and mortar. The Church is made up of living stones, people who have been quickened or made alive through Christ (*Ephesians 2:5*). The building materials come together to form the house of God only as they become vitally identified with the cornerstone. Many have tried to become a part of God's house while rejecting the cornerstone. Their efforts are always futile because God says, "See, I am sending Christ to be the carefully chosen, precious Cornerstone . . . The same Stone that was rejected by the builders has become the Cornerstone' . . . 'He is the Stone that some will stumble over, and the Rock that will make them fall.' They will stumble because they will not listen to God's Word" (*1 Peter 2:6-8, The Living Bible*).

24 MARCH

PRIDE'S DOWNWARD PULL—2 SAMUEL
(eight days to read)
"And Thou dost save an afflicted people; But Thine eyes are

on the haughty whom Thou dost abase" (*2 Samuel 22:28*).

"When pride cometh, then cometh shame" (*Proverbs 11:2*). Watch this principle operate as you read about David's life in 2 Samuel.

David's sin of carelessness in gathering many wives was the first indication of pride. Then, instead of leading his armies in war he stayed behind in Jerusalem. His conceit dulled his conscience. Then when temptation struck he fell. The third step down was cowardice. His heart was calloused to where he tried to cover his first evil deed by committing a second.

If David, a man after God's own heart, was taken by pride, we had better be careful.

25 MARCH

"Having been built upon the foundation of the apostles and prophets" (*Ephesians 2:20*).

Jesus Christ is the cornerstone of the foundation of the Church. His apostles and prophets are part of the foundation. The Church is built upon them. The apostles referred to here are the ones Jesus Christ specifically selected and equipped for the task of starting the building. They had a unique place in the plan of God. The Bible provides no indication that the apostolate with its authority was transmitted to subsequent leaders. The same can be said for the prophets referred to here. These were men gifted of God to proclaim His message, including predictive elements. When the Word of God was completed, their unique function was no more necessary. The foundation was finished. The building continues to be built.

In a general sense a missionary or pioneer church planter is an apostle. The root meaning of apostle is "sent one." It is also true that there are prophets in the church today, gifted of God to tell forth the message of God. Paul said, "Pursue love, yet desire earnestly spiritual gifts, but especially that you may prophesy" (*1 Corinthians 14:1*). Neither of these callings, however, entitles one to add to or adjust the written Word of God. They must function within what God has already revealed in His Word.

26 MARCH

"In whom the whole building, being fitted together is growing into a holy temple in the Lord; in whom you also are being built together into a dwelling of God in the Spirit" (*Ephesians 2:21, 22*).

The Church is growing into a holy temple. At times she grows faster than others. Sometimes it seems as though alterations are necessary in the process of her becoming all that God intends for her to be. To be a dwelling place for God puts a special demand on her. The Church must be holy. The ultimate factor in producing holiness is the precious blood of Jesus Christ. To be a part of this building you must believe that the blood of Jesus Christ, shed while dying for our sins, is the basis upon which God atones for our sins. We are forgiven and cleansed when through faith we trust Christ to be our Savior. We continue to be cleansed as we continue to walk in the light and confess every sin we become aware of in our lives (*1 John 1:7-10*).

Another cleansing agent is God's Word. The Psalmist said, "Wherewithal shall a young man cleanse his way? By taking heed thereto according to Thy Word" (*Psalms 119:9, KJV*). The Church must be a place where the sacrifice Jesus Christ made is always remembered and referred to. She must also focus her attention on the Word of God. Only then will she be a holy temple in the Lord and a place fit for God's dwelling.

27 MARCH

"That He might present to Himself the church in all her glory, having no spot or wrinkle or any such thing; but that she should be holy and blameless" (*Ephesians 5:27*).

This is the grand and glorious goal Jesus Christ has in mind for His Church. The Church is not there yet. She still has some ugly spots and persistent wrinkles. There are things for which she stands blameable. She is not holy. But God is not through with His Church. He is melting and purifying and molding her day by day.

I have had the privilege of traveling to many parts of the world and fellowshiping with many different members of the body of Christ. Flaws are obvious everywhere. At times I as a pastor wonder if God can ever transform His church to be acceptable to His high and holy standard. But at the same time, it is clear that God is at work. He allows difficulties, if not persecution, to bring deficiencies and disobedience into focus. He deals firmly with stubborn resistance. He withdraws the manifestation of His presence when His people compromise with the world. Then, in mercy and love, He moves in mysterious ways to convict, convince, correct, and draw His people back to Himself. Paul, writing with great confidence, affirms, "He who began a good work in you will perfect it until the day of Christ Jesus" (*Philippians 1:6*).

28 MARCH

"And now, little children, abide in Him so that if He should appear, we may have confidence and not shrink away from Him in shame at His coming" (*1 John 2:28*).

John is not suggesting a possibility that Christ will not appear. The word "if" refers not to the fact but to the time

of Christ's coming. It could be translated "whenever He
appears." We should always be abiding in Christ,
maintaining open and intimate fellowship with Him, so
that when He appears we will be ready to meet Him. Enoch
is a good example of what John is saying. The Bible
declares, "And Enoch walked with God; and he was not, for
God took him" (*Genesis 5:24*). The transition from walking
with God on earth to being taken by God into another state
was smooth and natural. John says "we may have
confidence" if we are ready to meet the Lord.

On the other hand, if you are not ready when Christ
returns, you will "shrink away from Him in shame."
Vincent says, "The fundamental thought is that of *separation*
and *shrinking* from God through the shame of conscious
guilt."⁹ This is in total contrast to the testimony of the
apostle Paul to Timothy: "I have fought the good fight, I
have finished the course, I have kept the faith; in the future
there is laid up for me the crown of righteousness, which
the Lord, the righteous Judge, will award to me on that
day; and not only to me, but also to all who have loved His
appearing" (*2 Timothy 4:7, 8*). Let Paul's testimony be an
encouragement and John's warning a challenge.

9. *Op. cit., Wuest, In These Last Days, pp.*
139, 140.

29 MARCH

*"For we must all appear before the judgment-
seat of Christ" (2 Corinthians 5:10).*

It is true that we have not been appointed unto God's
wrath. We need not fear eternal damnation if we are God's
children through faith in Jesus Christ. We will not be
judged before the great white throne (*Revelation 20:11-15*).
We are accepted in the Beloved (*Ephesians 1:3-6*). But don't
allow these assurances to make you irresponsible in your
Christian conduct and service.

When Christ returns for His own, at the rapture, and
takes them to Himself, there will take place a judgment of
believers before the judgment-seat of Christ. There are many
different ideas about just what will happen in this event.
Some feel there will be much sorrow and sadness there as
Christ reveals the sins of commission and omission which
have not been confessed in this life. Others feel it won't be
that way because there will be no more tears in glory
(*Revelation 21:4*). Paul simply states that Christians will
appear at this judgment in order "that each one may be
recompensed for his deeds in the body, according to what he
has done, whether good or bad" (*2 Corinthians 5:10*). What
we are like in our lifetime here on earth will have an effect
on how we will be recompensed on that day. We should,
therefore, always live with that day in mind.

30 MARCH

*"Each man's work will become evident; for the
day will show it, because it is to be revealed
with fire; and the fire itself will test the quality of each
man's work"* (*1 Corinthians 3:13*).

This fiery test is related to the judgment-seat of Christ.
When we appear before Him, all that we have done will be
tested. The focus here is not on quantity, but on quality.
That is not to say God is not interested in how much you
do for Him. He is. But whatever you do for Him must be
quality work or it will be worthless.

The foundation is Jesus Christ. We must take care what
and with what we build on that foundation. What we do
for God is here pictured by the different building materials:
"gold, silver, precious stones, wood, hay, straw"
(*1 Corinthians 3:12*). Enduring quality is what God is
looking for. Fire is the test which must be endured. Fire
consumes. It also purifies. That which endures the test of
fire will earn a reward (*1 Corinthians 3:14*). If what we have

done is likened to materials which are consumed in the fiery test, then we will have labored in vain and will not receive a reward (*1 Corinthians 3:15*).

Make sure you understand the focus in this discussion. Paul points out that even if you suffer the loss of all possible rewards, you cannot as a Christian lose your salvation by failure in service. Salvation is not as a result of works (*Ephesians 2:8, 9*).

31 MARCH

"But if we judged ourselves rightly, we should not be judged" (*1 Corinthians 11:31*).

When Paul here says, "if we judged ourselves," he means, "if we discerned ourselves," or examined and formed a right estimate of ourselves. In the context, he is not referring here to making a proper discernment about whether or not we are saved (note verse 32). He is talking about living in such a way that if something is wrong in our relationship with God or man, we see to it that the wrong is made right through confession and restoration where necessary. If we indeed did this on a regular basis "we should not be judged." Nor would we "shrink away from Him in shame at His coming."

God does not judge what already has been judged. Whenever we deal with sin as the Holy Spirit convicts us about it, God graciously forgives and cleanses. He will not bring up again what He has already forgiven. It is wiped out of the record. We need not be concerned about it being brought up at the judgment-seat of Christ. If on the other hand we neglect or refuse to respond to the conviction of the Holy Spirit, God will deal with us firmly in this life, even to the degree that our life may be shortened (*1 Corinthians 11:30*). And be assured, refusal to respond to the conviction of the Holy Spirit will affect the evaluation of one's life at the judgment-seat of Christ.

1 APRIL

THE TRAGEDY OF MISUSED PRIVILEGE—
1 KINGS (nine days to read)

*"For it came about when Solomon was old, his wives
turned his heart away after other gods; and his heart was
not wholly devoted to the Lord his God, as the heart of
David his father had been" (1 Kings 11:4).*

Misused privilege is the greatest of tragedies.

God made Solomon a wise and winsome king. Everything
he put his hands to prospered. At first he used his assets
wisely, but soon God's gifts became more important to him
than God Himself. Solomon became careless, and before he
knew it he failed. His many wives, who worshiped false
gods, led him into idolatry.

What Solomon started, his successors in the divided
kingdom continued. And they plunged Israel down to ruin.

Whenever we put God's gift before God Himself we reap
the poverty of the perishable and experience the doom of
God's rejection. Always remember that God demands first
place, for He is a jealous God.

2 APRIL

*"The Lord God, the Almighty"
(Revelation 4:8).*

More than fifty times the Lord God is designated in the
Bible as the Almighty. The Bible is a record of His mighty
acts. From creation on, everything which exists is subject to
His authority and control. He gave it being. He set the
boundaries of its being.

Man in his puny arrogance often asserts his own will.
He feels he has a right to his freedom, and can set the
limits of his freedom. God, however, is the only One who
is truly free. If He wanted to, He could make the earth as
barren as the moon and as uninhabitable. He once moved

in power to judge the earth and her inhabitants, calling forth the waters of the deep and thundering down rains from above. Once He extended the time of day. Another time, He turned time back an hour. The Almighty has the right and the power to do what He chooses.

The Bible talks of a day yet to come in which He will bring to pass judgments that are of such a phenomenal nature that they boggle the imagination. It is a fool who says, "there is no God." It is a greater fool who opposes the Almighty. God as God will not fail in what He sets out to accomplish.

3 APRIL

"Is anything too difficult for the Lord?"
(*Genesis 18:14*).

Abraham and his wife Sarah had a hard time believing that the Almighty was indeed able to perform the miracle of giving them a son in their old age. They had believed at one time when they were younger. The older they got, the less probable the promise became. No doubt God waited until it was too late from a human standpoint for Sarah to bear a child. Then God reaffirmed His promise and posed the above question. The obvious answer, since God is Almighty, is a resounding "No!"

Job, after many days of struggle, declared, "I know that Thou canst do all things" (*Job 42:2*). When Jesus Christ explained the difficulty of a rich man being saved, His disciples asked Him who could be saved. His answer was, "With men this is impossible, but with God all things are possible" (*Matthew 19:26*). When Mary questioned the possibility of giving birth to the Savior without having known a man, the angel, Gabriel, answered, "Behold, even your relative Elizabeth has also conceived a son in her old age; and she who was called barren is now in her sixth month. For nothing will be impossible with God" (*Luke 1:36, 37*).

No matter what you face today, or any day for the rest of your life, you can rest assured that with God nothing is too difficult or too great or too powerful for Him to overcome. He is omnipotent, all-powerful.

4 APRIL

"Now to Him who is able to do exceeding abundantly beyond all that we ask or think . . ." (*Ephesians 3:20*).

Paul here stretches human language to awkward limits in order to expand his readers' minds to grasp something of the greatness of God's power. Dr. Kenneth Wuest explains the statement as follows, referring to the Greek words:

"In this doxology, we have two descriptions of God—one, a general one; the other, one that is specific and has to do with believers. The first characterizes Him as One who is able to do . . . literally, 'above all things,' thus, 'in a measure exceeding all things, beyond all things.' The second . . . is made up of [two words. The first one speaks of] 'exceeding some number or measure, over and above, more than necessary.' [The second] is perfective in force here, intensifying the already existing idea in the verb, here adding the idea of exhaustlessness, and . . .'above.' The compound word is a superlative of superlatives in force. It speaks of the ability of God to do something, that ability having more than enough potential power, this power exhaustless, and then some on top of that. Thus, Paul says that God is able to do super-abundantly above and beyond what we ask or think, and then some on top of that."[10]

10. *Op. cit., Wuest, Ephesians and Colossians, p. 91.*

5 APRIL

"Then the Lord said to Satan, 'Behold, all that he has is in your power, only do not put forth your hand on him.' So Satan departed from the presence of the Lord" (Job 1:12).

Many wonder why God does not totally destroy Satan. Nor is it easy to understand why, if God doesn't destroy Satan, He at least does not restrain his evil activities more. God gave Satan permission to do what he wanted with all that Job possessed. Later God gave even greater freedom: "Behold, he is in your power. Only spare his life" (*Job 2:6*). Satan took every inch God allowed him, and Job went through excruciating suffering as a result. Why did God allow it?

One thing that can be said first is that God *did* allow it. Had He not allowed it, Satan could not have done what he did. God is more powerful than Satan and, therefore, has the prerogative to set boundaries beyond which Satan cannot go. Satan is absolutely subject to God's will and word. Should he try to go beyond what God wills, he would be resisted successfully by the power of God. Though it at times seems Satan is gaining the upper hand, we need not fear. "For the Lord our God, the Almighty, reigns" (*Revelation 19:6*).

Though we don't always understand how He does it, "we know that in all things God works for the good of those who love Him, who have been called according to His purpose" (*Romans 8:28, NIV*). There is nothing God cannot do, but He limits Himself by the exercise of His wisdom as revealed in His will. He does or allows to be done only what His love and wisdom dictate.

6 APRIL

"He . . . upholds all things by the word of His power" (Hebrews 1:3).

Jesus Christ created all that was created. As the Creator, He has authority over all that was created. It is subject to His beck and call. When the disciples were afraid in the storm-tossed boat, Jesus Christ rebuked their lack of faith, then calmly turned to the storm and demanded that the wind and sea become calm. They did immediately. He was able to multiply a few loaves and fish to feed a great multitude. He was unlimited in His power over the natural world.

Referring to Hebrews 1:3, Dr. Wuest comments: "This act has to do, not only with sustaining the weight of the universe, but also with maintaining its coherence and carrying on its development. Paul speaks of this same act of the Son in Colossians 1:17 where he says, 'By Him all things consist.' That is, all things maintain their coherence in Him. The Lord Jesus holds all things together and in their proper relationship to each other by His own power. The oceans are held in their beds. The rivers run down into the sea. The heavenly bodies are held in their orbits. Philo calls the Logos the bond of the universe. This act of maintaining this coherence, implies the guidance and propulsion of all the parts of the universe to a definite end."[11]

11. *Kenneth Wuest, Word Studies in the Greek New Testament, Book 13, Hebrews (Grand Rapids: Eerdmans, © 1947), p. 39. Used by permission.*

7 APRIL

"Truly, truly, I say to you, an hour is coming and now is, when the dead shall hear the voice of the Son of God; and those who hear shall live" (John 5:25).

It is obvious when you read the Gospel narratives on the life of Jesus Christ that He acted as one with authority and power. When confronted by the blind, the lame, the deaf and dumb, and the diseased, He unflinchingly reached out to heal and help. At times multitudes were brought to Him for healing. No matter what illness He encountered, He was able to deliver the sufferer if He willed it. He could heal even when separated from the sufferer as in the case of the ruler's son (*John 4:46-54*).

Even more amazing than the many incidents of healing are the stirring accounts of Jesus Christ raising people from the dead. He raised the daughter of Jairus (*Mark 5:41, 42*), the only son of a woman of Nain (*Luke 7:14*), and Lazarus (*John 11:43*). In the case of Lazarus, He deliberately waited, not only for Lazarus to die, but to be buried for a few days before He arrived to perform the miracle of raising him from the dead. Sickness and death obviously are subject to His authority. They cannot resist His power.

8 APRIL

"And demons also were coming out of many, crying out and saying, 'You are the Son of God!' And rebuking them, He would not allow them to speak, because they knew Him to be the Christ" (*Luke 4:41*).

Another area in which Jesus Christ demonstrated His omnipotence is in His relationship to Satan and his host of evil partners. Satan was no match for Jesus Christ in the wilderness temptations. Every evil power Jesus Christ confronted was subject to His authority. When Jesus Christ commanded demons to depart from various ones, they had no choice but to obey.

The promise God made in Genesis 3:15, "He [Jesus Christ] shall bruise you [Satan] on the head," was gloriously fulfilled on the cross where Jesus Christ won our salvation. Paul declares this victory over Satan and his kingdom in

Colossians 2:15: "He thus stripped the principalities and dominions of power and made a public display of them, triumphing over them by the cross" (*Williams*). Paul also said in another place that Jesus Christ is exalted "far, far above any other king or ruler or dictator or leader . . . God has put all things under his feet" (*Ephesians 1:21, 22, The Living Bible*).

9 APRIL

"The Father is greater than I" (*John 14:28*).

This is a rather startling statement made by Jesus Christ to His disciples. He was sharing the fact that He was going to die, and after His resurrection go back to be with His Father in heaven. If the disciples really understood what Jesus was saying, they would have rejoiced. But they thought Jesus was the ultimate answer, the end of all their hopes. Jesus had to correct their erroneous thinking and cause them to look beyond Himself in the flesh.

Jesus did not mean that He was less than His Father in His essential being. That would contradict His statement in John 10:30: "I and the Father are one." Jesus was referring to the position He assumed in His incarnation when He "emptied Himself, taking the form of a bondservant, and being made in the likeness of man" (*Philippians 2:7*). When Jesus Christ agreed to this act of self-emptying, God the Father sent Him on His mission. He was begotten of the Father when the Holy Spirit overshadowed Mary and she conceived. This was in fulfillment of Psalm 2:7, "Thou art My Son, today I have begotten Thee." In His earthly sojourn, Jesus Christ was subordinate to the Father.

10 APRIL

OUR MAP AND MANDATE—2 KINGS
(six days to read)

"'If the people of Israel will only follow the instructions I gave them through Moses, I will never again expel them from this land of their fathers.' But the people did not listen to the Lord" (2 Kings 21:8, 9, The Living Bible).

"Sin will keep you from the Bible or the Bible will keep you from sin." So said D. L. Moody. Israel's history as recorded in 2 Kings vividly portrays this.

As brightly shining lights, Elisha, Hezekiah, and Josiah break through the dismal scene of Israel's road to ruin. Even though the tide of sin was against them, they stood alone for what was right. How? By making God's Word the map and mandate for their lives. This is God's answer for our need when confronted or opposed by evil.

Therefore, delight yourself in the Bible and meditate on what it says day and night (*Psalm 1:2*). Hide its truth in your heart and you will be kept from sinning against God (*Psalm 119:11*).

11 APRIL

"Greater is He who is in you than he who is in the world" (1 John 4:4).

We have already seen that God the Father and God the Son are omnipotent. One area in which we considered their authority and power was that of their domination over the evil kingdom of Satan. In the above statement, John declares that God the Holy Spirit is also greater than Satan and his cohorts.

If left to ourselves, Satan would be able to master us. He is greater, wiser, more powerful than we are. But when we become children of God through faith in Jesus Christ the Holy Spirit comes to dwell within us. He becomes our

constant companion and comforter. He also becomes our
protector. In divine power, He overcomes the wiles and
attacks of Satan. He promises to bring us through all enemy
forces.

All we need do is trust in His guiding and keeping
power. Paul encourages Timothy with the promise, "For
the Holy Spirit, God's gift, does not want you to be afraid,
but to be wise and strong" (*2 Timothy 1:7, The Living
Bible*). We should walk out into the world each day
confident that the Holy Spirit's presence will enable us to
conquer every attack of the enemy.

12 APRIL

*"The Helper, the Holy Spirit, whom the Father
will send in My name" (John 14:26).*

We have seen that though Jesus Christ is equal with the
Father in their essential being, He is subordinate to the
Father in certain functions. The Father sent the Son into the
world. Similarly, the Father sent the Holy Spirit to fulfill a
function in the world.

As to their essential being, the Holy Spirit is one with the
Father and the Son. But He is obviously subordinate to the
Father in function. Furthermore, He is subordinate to the
Son in function. Jesus Christ promised the disciples, "When
the Helper comes, whom I will send to you from the Father,
that is the Spirit of truth, who proceeds from the Father, He
will bear witness of Me" (*John 15:26*). Jesus Christ sent the
Holy Spirit to bear witness of Him and to glorify Him
(*John 16:14*).

The Spirit speaks what both the Father and the Son
indicate should be said. In Romans 8:9, He is referred to
both as "the Spirit of God" and "the Spirit of Christ." We
must underline, however, the fact that though the Son is in
this way functionally subordinate to the Father, and the

Holy Spirit is functionally subordinate to the Father and the Son, in a unique way, far beyond human comprehension, they are fully equal, the blessed holy Trinity.

13 APRIL

"And God blessed them; and God said to them, 'Be fruitful and multiply, and fill the earth, and subdue it; and rule over the fish of the sea and over the birds of the sky, and over every living thing that moves on the earth'" (Genesis 1:28).

Man is the highest of the created beings referred to in the creation account in Genesis. God blessed Adam and Eve and commanded them to subdue and rule over all else which was created. To do this effectively, man would need to possess superiority over the other created beings. In this sense man has significant power.

Over the years of human history, man has demonstrated his ability to accomplish fantastic feats of power. Consider the ancient Egyptian pyramids, the remains of the ancient Inca civilization, and other phenomena of human achievement. In our present day man has made great strides in scientific accomplishment by developing nuclear power, traveling to the moon, and sending probes to distant planets.

The problem man faces, however, is that he often doesn't progress in his ability to utilize his accomplishments for the benefit of humanity. Pollution has increased to the danger point in many parts of the world. Morality runs at such a low ebb that man's advances become submerged in his degenerating drift. Man is powerful, but without a proper relationship with God that power backfires and man destroys himself.

14 APRIL

"Apart from Me you can do nothing" (John 15:5).

This is a humbling but true conclusion Jesus Christ wants every one of us to come to. Man, though powerful, is incapable of accomplishing anything of eternal value without being associated with Jesus Christ. He becomes man's source of victory.

Paul the apostle concluded, "I know I am rotten through and through so far as my old sinful nature is concerned. No matter which way I turn I can't make myself do right. I want to but I can't. When I want to do good, I don't; and when I try not to do wrong, I do it anyway" (*Romans 7:18, 19, The Living Bible*).

What good is the intention to do good if we do not have the ability to carry out our intentions? What good is accomplishment in any and every other area of life if we cannot fulfill moral objectives? What good is the ability to subdue the earth and rule over all that is in the world, if we can't subdue our own evil hearts and rule them in conformity to God's will? Paul cries out, "Wretched man that I am! Who will set me free from the body of this death?" (*Romans 7:24*).

15 APRIL

"For while we were still helpless, at the right time Christ died for the ungodly" (Romans 5:6).

The word "helpless" refers to man's utter inability to work out his own salvation. He is without strength in that matter. All he does results in failure. He is, therefore, without hope. Trying to please God under these circumstances is futile.

Knowing our weakness, God at the right time sent His Son to do for us what we could not do for ourselves. We could not remove the load of sin. "Christ died for the ungodly," thus taking the load of our sin on Himself. He bore our sins away, carrying them up to the cross (*1 Peter 2:24*). This is the *grace* of God: God doing for us what we were incapable of doing. What is impossible with man is possible with God. We are impotent. He is omnipotent.

The preaching of this glorious truth is foolishness to those who do not believe. To those who by faith receive it as true, it is the power of God unto salvation (*1 Corinthians 1:18*).

16 APRIL

ON GETTING AND GIVING—
1 CHRONICLES (eight days to read)

"And David said, 'My son Solomon is young and inexperienced, and the house that is to be built for the Lord shall be exceedingly magnificent, famous and glorious throughout all lands. Therefore I will make preparation for it.' So David made ample preparations before his death"
(*1 Chronicles 22:5*).

Long ago a traveler came upon an elderly man planting fruit trees. "You are very old," said the traveler, "and it will be many years before these begin to bear. You can't expect to enjoy them."

"Oh, yes, I can," said the gray-haired man. "I am drawing pleasure from them now in anticipation." Then, pointing to another section of his land, he asked, "Do you see those fruit-laden trees? My father planted them for me to enjoy, and now I'm planting these for my children."

When David realized the consequences of his selfishness and pride, he confessed his sin to God and was forgiven. Then he realized that to whom much has been given of him shall much be required (*Luke 12:48*).

God promised David that his son would build the temple. David responded by providing the materials and men needed to do the job. And because of this preparation his dream and desire to see a temple of God erected in Jerusalem came true. Consequently his life demonstrates the principle: it is more blessed to give than to get!

17 APRIL

"But if it is by grace, it is no longer on the basis of works, otherwise grace is no longer grace" (Romans 11:6).

We have seen already that though man has great resources, he is impotent when it comes to saving himself. Without Christ it is impossible for man to achieve anything of eternal significance. There are some, however, who feel that with Christ's help they can do what is necessary to achieve salvation—Christ does some things for us which we can't do for ourselves, but there are some things we can and must do. Usually they refer to James 2:26 as a basis for this view: "Faith without works is dead."

Paul, however, points out that if I must add to what Christ has done, then Christ's work was not complete and grace would be no more grace. In fact, Paul says works and grace are mutually exclusive. You cannot mix them.

A Christian was trying to win a cabinetmaker to faith in Christ. The cabinetmaker, however, thought he had to do something too. One day the Christian was in his shop. He picked up a plane, went over to a finished cabinet, and acted as though he was going to use the plane on the top surface. "Stop! You'll spoil it!" the cabinetmaker shouted. "That surface is finished!"

The Christian then graciously pointed out, "That's the way it is with salvation. It is a finished work of Christ. If you try to do anything more than what He has done, you will only spoil it." To be saved we must accept the perfect, finished work of Christ.

18 APRIL

"For by grace you have been saved through faith; and that not of yourselves. It is the gift of God; not as a result of works, that no one should boast" *(Ephesians 2:8, 9).*

Salvation as presented in the Bible is a gift. It is not something for which we can work in order to earn it. Nor is it something for which you can pay. Never will you be able to merit it. Remember, we are all like sheep who have gone astray by going our own way *(Isaiah 53:6)*. All of us have sinned *(Romans 3:23)*. As sinners, we are incapable of measuring up to what alone would be acceptable to a holy God.

Salvation is the gift of God. It is a gift of inestimable value. As unworthy as we are, we have the privilege and opportunity to experience salvation when we receive it as a gift by faith. There is no room or ground for boasting on our part. God will not share His glory with anyone. In simple, humble faith we must reach out and receive all that God has graciously done for us. When we do, we are saved. "But as many as received Him, to them He gave the right to become children of God, even to those who believe in His name: who were born not of blood, nor of the will of the flesh, nor of the will of man, but of God" *(John 1:12, 13)*.

19 APRIL

"Without faith it is impossible to please Him, for he who comes to God must believe that He is, and that He is a rewarder of those who seek Him" *(Hebrews 11:6)*.

Faith is the key which opens the door of salvation. Without it we cannot please God. Faith is indispensable to salvation. It is important, therefore, to understand what and how we must believe.

Jesus spoke of people who believed but to whom He would not commit Himself *(John 2:23, 24)*. Why? Because He knew what was in man. Theirs was obviously a deficient faith. James writes about devils who believe, but who tremble in their resistance *(James 2:19)*.

We must believe that God is. It would be meaningless to believe merely in a good concept or idea. He is. He has being. He is real. And we must believe that He also is a rewarder of those who diligently seek Him. Faith expects a response from God. It is not a fatalistic leap into the dark. It is a coming to God who is waiting for us with outstretched hands ready to embrace us. Faith doesn't rest until it rests embraced in the bosom of the Father. Joanie Yoder, in a missionary newsletter, shared how Paul's words concerning walking by faith, not sight, had taken on new meaning for her. Paul was not saying "faith *instead* of sight." He was saying "faith *until* sight." Joanie summarized her insight: "Faith is the waiting room of sight."

20 APRIL

"Now faith is the assurance of things hoped for, the conviction of things not seen" (Hebrews 11:1).

This chapter of Hebrews records some of what was accomplished through a number of those who had faith in Old Testament times. The writer begins his presentation with a definition of faith. It is important to understand this definition clearly since all the illustrations following in this chapter are built upon it. Vincent believes "the key is furnished by verse 27, as *seeing him who is invisible.* Faith apprehends as a real fact what is not revealed to the senses. It rests on that fact, acts upon it, and is upheld by it in the face of all that seems to contradict it. Faith is real seeing."[12]

Looking more closely at the words *assurance* and *conviction,* commentators Moulton and Milligan indicate that *assurance* is a legal term which stands for "the whole body of documents bearing on the ownership of a person's property, deposited in archives, and forming the evidence of ownership."[13] With this in mind, they suggest the first part of the definition be translated, "Faith is the title-deed of things hoped for."[14]

The word translated *conviction* in this instance means "a proof, that by which a thing is proved or tested." Thayer defines it in this context as "that by which invisible things are proved and we are convinced of their reality."[15] Faith gives stability, assurance, and inner conviction concerning all things which are not open to the physical senses, especially in the realm of salvation.

12. *Op.cit., Wuest, Hebrews, p. 193.*
13. *Ibid.*
14. *Ibid.*
15. *Ibid.*

21 APRIL

"God has allotted to each a measure of faith" (Romans 12:3).

Salvation is a gift of God which we are to receive by faith (*Romans 6:23*). Sanctification, living wholly for God, is also a gift of God entered into and experienced by faith (*Romans 6:11*). Spiritual gifts for service are exercised by faith (*Romans 12:6*). The obvious dynamic of spiritual prosperity is found in the promise of Jesus Christ: "Be it done to you according to your faith" (*Matthew 9:29*).

Having said all this, we must always keep in mind that it is God who allots or gives to each a measure of faith. Faith is a gift of God. Jesus Christ is "the author and perfecter of faith." We must fix "our eyes on Jesus" (*Hebrews 12:2*). It is as though looking toward the Giver is all that we can do. Looking with beseeching eyes. This is no doubt why Paul "determined to know nothing" among the Corinthians, "except Jesus Christ, and Him crucified" (*1 Corinthians*

2:2). This is also why the Holy Spirit seeks to glorify Christ (*John 16:14*). For when Jesus Christ is lifted up for all to view, He will draw all to Himself (*John 12:32*).

22 APRIL

"Faith comes from hearing, and hearing by the word of Christ" (Romans 10:17).

Faith to many is an illusive thing. They don't feel they have faith and they don't know how to get it. Paul emphasizes the importance of believers sending forth the message of Christ, because one will only call on Christ for salvation when it is known that He is able and available to save (*Romans 10:13-16*). Then Paul declares that faith comes as a result of hearing the gospel message. All that is necessary is hearing. When we hear, it is as though the seed of faith is planted in our hearts. As we continue hearing, that seed germinates and ultimately bursts forth as a living faith.

In other words, faith is not an inherent characteristic in our lives. It is something which comes to us when we make ourselves receptive to the Word about Christ. To some, faith "comes" readily. To others it "comes" gradually over a long period of time. But to all who would have faith, it "comes" from hearing the Word about Christ. So if you want faith initially and increasingly, you must take seriously the words of Christ, "He who has ears to hear, let him hear" (*Matthew 11:15*).

23 APRIL

"Many of those who had heard the message believed" (Acts 4:4).

Over and over again this is recorded to show how faith

was imparted. When Paul and Silas told the Philippian jailer to believe on the Lord Jesus Christ and he would be saved, they immediately proceeded to speak the word of the Lord unto him (*Acts 16:31, 32*).

If you want to become mighty in believing prayer you must search in God's Word for promises that are related to your requests. Then meditate upon them and as it were pray them back to God. This process is a faith builder. And if you want to help someone else grow in faith, share with them the promises which have helped you. You can pray all you want to for faith, but if you don't give faith its proper nourishment it won't grow, just as praying for health while refusing to partake of nourishing food does us no good.

24 APRIL

FRIEND OR FOE—2 CHRONICLES
(eleven days to read)

"And he did evil in the sight of the Lord like the house of Ahab, for they were his counselors after the death of his father, to his destruction" (*2 Chronicles 22:4*).

One springtime, crows began to pull up a certain farmer's young corn. Loading his gun, he went out to frighten them away. This same man had a parrot which, when he saw the crows, went over and joined them. When the farmer finished shooting, he found to his surprise that besides killing three crows he had also wounded his pet.

"What did it, Daddy? What hurt our pretty Polly?" cried his children when he arrived home with their bedraggled pet.

The farmer answered solemnly, "Bad company! Bad company!"

King Solomon counsels us, "He that walketh with wise men shall be wise: but a companion of fools shall be destroyed" (*Proverbs 13:20*). We must be careful that the one who poses as a friend is not a foe in disguise. A study of the companions of the kings of Judah in 2 Chronicles will constructively confirm this warning. For many of the kings were deceived and defeated by foes posing as friends.

The best way to find a true friend is to walk with God yourself and choose your friends from among those who walk with God. Your companions will either make or break you.

25 APRIL

"I remind you to kindle afresh the gift of God which is in you" (2 Timothy 1:6).

Timothy was a man gifted of God for service. By the grace of God he was given important leadership responsibility. In that responsibility, however, he evidently did not exercise his gift. It was lying dormant. Because of this, the church in Ephesus, which he oversaw, suffered. Paul, therefore, reminds Timothy that he should kindle afresh the gift of God which was in him. Once God gives a gift, He does not take it away. "The gifts of God are irrevocable" (*Romans 11:29*).

True humility does not hide its light under a bushel. It lets the light shine forth where needed, always giving glory to the One who makes it possible. Similarly, true humility does not hide the gift received from God. It exercises it for the benefit of others, but always gives the glory to the one who provided the gift.

Dr. Wuest, my Greek teacher in Bible school, used to tell us that whenever he was praised for his work for the Lord, "I always send the bouquets up to heaven." That is precisely what Peter meant when he wrote, "As each one has received a special gift, employ it in serving one another, as good stewards of the manifold grace of God. Whoever speaks, let him speak, as it were, the utterances of God; whoever serves, let him do so as by the strength which God supplies; so that in all things God may be glorified through Jesus Christ to whom belongs the glory and dominion forever and ever" (*1 Peter 4:10, 11*).

26 APRIL

"Since we have gifts that differ according to the grace given to us, let each exercise them accordingly: if prophecy, according to the proportion of his faith" (Romans 12:6).

When one becomes a believer, God not only draws him into a new relationship with Himself, God places him into the body of Christ by His Spirit. This is the baptizing work of the Holy Spirit (*1 Corinthians 12:13*). By thus becoming a member in the body of Christ, he has a new relationship to those who are also members of the body of Christ. They are brothers and sisters, mutually dependent on one another and all together dependent on their head, Jesus Christ.

To each member is given a spiritual gift or gifts to be used to enrich the life and ministry of the whole body. God gives the gifts in grace. Each member must exercise his gift. But the way in which he exercises it is "according to the proportion of his faith." Some are gifted greatly, but exercise little faith in using their gift. Others are less gifted but exercise great faith in using their gift. Since God allots to each the measure of faith (*Romans 12:3*), we can conclude that as in salvation, so in service—God does it all.

If everyone in the body discovered his gift(s) from God and exercised those gift(s) according to the proportion of his faith, the body would grow in stature and influence at an amazing rate.

27 APRIL

"Each one has received a special gift"
(1 Peter 4:10).

We are reminded in a number of Bible portions that everyone who is a Christian is given at least one spiritual gift which he is to exercise for the edifying and building up of the body of Christ. It is obvious that many Christians are unaware of their spiritual gift, let alone using it. This is tragic for them and for the Church.

Some might ask, "How does one discover what his spiritual gift is?" Checking the Bible to understand what all the gifts are in order to familiarize yourself with them is a good first step (*Romans 12; 1 Corinthians 12; Ephesians 4:11; 1 Peter 4:10*).

Evaluating each gift in the list to determine what gift or gifts interest you is another step not too difficult to take. Prayer for the Holy Spirit's guidance and prompting is the next logical step. Then you should experiment in the area of the gift(s) you feel God may have chosen to give you. Another source of guidance is the counsel and/or encouragement of fellow believers who might see a certain potential you are unaware of.

If teaching emerges as a potential gift, look for an opportunity to teach. If administration, then look for an opportunity to lead. Always evaluate your attempts and be open for the criticism of others. Never stop being a learner. If you are gifted to teach, endeavor to become the best teacher you can possibly be. That should be true no matter what gift you have. Remember, your gift is a gift. It is entrusted to you for you to use. Be a responsible, faithful steward of all that God has entrusted to you.

28 APRIL

"You are not lacking in any gift . . . And I,
brethren, could not speak to you as to spiritual
men, but as to men of flesh, as to babes in Christ"
(1 Corinthians 1:7; 3:1).

Many gifted Christians are ineffective in using their gifts
because they are carnal, not spiritual. The Corinthian
church is a prime example of this tragic condition. For your
gift to be used effectively, your life must manifest the fruit
of the Spirit. We must love if we want to serve God
acceptably. We must also be humble. This demands that we
do nothing through strife or vainglory, but in lowliness of
mind esteem others better than ourselves *(Philippians 2:3).*
Obedience to the Spirit's guidance in determining the *when,*
where, and *how* of using your gift is also very important.
All this is possible only as you are filled with the Holy
Spirit.

Self-effort and self-advancement are both diametrically
opposed to the spiritual exercise of spiritual gifts. A
Christlike life, resulting from a work of the Holy Spirit, will
make even the least gifted an effective, fruitful servant of the
Lord. God looks not for ability or inability, but for
availability. He works through yielded vessels.

29 APRIL

"Savage wolves will come in among you, not
sparing the flock; and from among your own
selves men will arise, speaking perverse things, to draw
away the disciples after them" (Acts 20:29, 30).

Paul is giving his last farewell to the leaders of the church
at Ephesus. He emphasizes their responsibilities as leaders.
Then he warns them of the dangers of heretical teachers
who could lead believers, even leaders, astray. Spiritually
gifted men are given to enrich and build the Church

(*Ephesians 4:11*). Satan, who is a deceiver from the beginning, tries pushing on the church counterfeit gifts, through false teachers.

Jesus called such teachers wolves in sheep's clothing. To remain strong and pure, a church must be on guard against those wolves. And to be on guard against them we must mature.

Paul says in Ephesians 4:11-16: "And He gave some as apostles, and some as prophets, and some as evangelists, and some as pastors and teachers, for the equipping of the saints for the work of service, to the building up of the body of Christ; until we all attain to the unity of the faith, and of the knowledge of the Son of God, to a mature man, to the measure of the stature which belongs to the fulness of Christ.

"As a result, we are no longer to be children, tossed here and there by waves, and carried about by every wind of doctrine, by the trickery of men, by craftiness in deceitful scheming; but speaking the truth in love, we are to grow up in all aspects into Him, who is the head, even Christ, from whom the whole body, being fitted and held together by that which every joint supplies, according to the proper working of each individual part, causes the growth of the body for the building up of itself in love."

30 APRIL

"Such men are false apostles, deceitful workers, disguising themselves as apostles of Christ. And no wonder, for even Satan disguises himself as an angel of light" (2 Corinthians 11:13, 14).

Satan is a crafty enemy of the church of Jesus Christ. He tries to destroy her from the outside through opposition or persecution. He also infiltrates the ranks of believers and finds willing people who become his dupes to carry out his deceitful schemes. It is utterly amazing how many are deceived by his "angel of light" disguise. Some of the most attractive, well-mannered, gracious, and winsome people are instruments in his hands to blind multitudes to the truth. And this happens in some of the best churches.

Often the distortion is not easily recognized. Messages preached and lessons taught sound so much like what we have always heard. But there is a hidden hook, inside the bait, which at the right time is designed to capture you.

We must test the spirits to see if they are of God (*1 John 4:1*). Paul warns Timothy, "The Spirit explicitly says that in later times some will fall away from the faith, paying attention to deceitful spirits and doctrines of demons" (*1 Timothy 4:1*). Beware of the teachings of demons!

1 MAY

*"God is light, and in Him there is no
darkness at all" (1 John 1:5).*

Darkness in this portion of the Bible refers to moral
deficiency or unholiness. Light refers to holiness. God is
holy and in Him is no moral deficiency. He is absolutely
holy. James calls Him "the Father of lights, with whom is
no shadow of turning" (*James 1:17, KJV*). There is not even
a slight shadow marring the blazing glory of His holiness.
In His essential being He is unapproachably holy.

We have a difficult time comprehending this attribute of
God because we live in a world tainted by the curse. We
consider whiteness in relative terms. This is whiter than
that. It is impossible for us to fully comprehend the absolute
whiteness of God's nature. No impurities or imperfections
can be found. Perfection is personified in Him. If we want
to think of God rightly, we must think of Him as holy.

Solomon, the author of most of the Proverbs, says, "The
knowledge of the Holy One is understanding" (*Proverbs
9:10*). No matter how difficult it is for us to understand this
attribute of God, we should on a regular basis give ourselves
to meditating on it. It is essential if we would worship God
aright.

2 MAY

*"Thine eyes are too pure to approve (look at)
evil, and Thou canst not look on wickedness
with favor" (Habakkuk 1:13).*

It is important for us to be reminded of the fact that
because God is holy, it is impossible for Him to have
anything to do with sin except to judge it and turn His
back on it. He cannot compromise with sin. John said, "If
we say we are his friends, but go on living in spiritual

darkness and sin, we are lying. But if we are living in the light of God's presence, just as Christ does, then we have wonderful fellowship and joy with each other, and the blood of Jesus his Son cleanses us from every sin" (*1 John 1:6, 7, The Living Bible*).

At times we might think that our lives are acceptable to God. And there is a sense in which we are accepted in the beloved, the Lord Jesus Christ. But both in the Bible and in church history those who drew closest to God also seemed to be more aware of the stark contrast between their uncleanness and God's holiness. Note Isaiah's description of an encounter with God (*Isaiah 6:1-5*). Daniel also experienced similar reactions (*Daniel 10:2-9*). In the New Testament, John the apostle had such an experience which he described in Revelation 1:12-17.

This is the basis of the agony of Christ on the cross when He was made sin for us. This is why He cried out, "My God, My God, why hast Thou forsaken Me?" (*Matthew 27:46*).

3 MAY

"You shall be holy, for I am holy" (*1 Peter 1:15, 16*).

The most basic reason for the Christian to live a holy life is that his God is holy. God's holiness demands our holiness if we are to fellowship with Him.

"The entire Mosaic system of washings; divisions of the tabernacle; divisions of the people into ordinary Israelites, Levites, Priests and High Priests, who were permitted different degrees of approach to God, under strictly defined conditions; the insisting upon sacrifice as a necessary medium of approach to God; God's directions to Moses in Exodus 3:5, to Joshua in Joshua 5:15, the punishment of Uzziah in 2 Chronicles 26:16-26; the strict orders to Israel in regard to approaching Sinai when Jehovah came down upon it; the doom of Korah, Dathan and Abiram in Numbers 16:1-33;

and the destruction of Nadab and Abihu in Leviticus 10:1-3; all these were intended to teach, emphasize and burn into the minds and hearts of the Israelites the fundamental truth that God is holy, unapproachably holy. The truth that God is holy is *the* fundamental truth of the Bible, of the Old Testament and the New Testament, of the Jewish Religion and the Christian Religion."[16]

16. *Op. cit., Torrey*, p. 37.

4 MAY

"The Lord is righteous in all His ways, and holy in all His works" (Psalm 145:17, KJV).

This is a reflection on God's character. He is all He claims to be. All He does is consistent with His claims. Nothing about Him is crooked or deceptive. You can count on what He has revealed about Himself and His works.

When the Psalmist affirms that the Lord is "holy in all His works," he is saying that whatever God does is done for a holy objective, with a holy motive, and in a holy manner. At times it might seem as though some compromise has infiltrated that holy triangle. That is only because we don't see things for what they really are. Don't try to find fault in what God does or the way He does it. None of us understand all the ramifications of the situation. God does. And He alone can deal with each facet of the issue in a righteous fashion.

5 MAY

SEPARATED TO SUCCEED—EZRA (three days to read)

"Now, therefore, make confession to the Lord God of your fathers, and do His will; and separate yourselves from the

peoples of the land and from the foreign wives" (*Ezra 10:11*).

After seventy years in captivity, Israel received from God another chance. Cyrus decreed that the temples in Jerusalem be rebuilt and provided the returning Israelites with the necessary materials.

When the work began, Israel's enemies deceitfully offered to help. But Israel wouldn't accept their offer. The enemies then had the work stopped by decree. After a time God's prophets persuaded the people to continue the work anyway, and before long the temple was completed.

In time Israel became careless and intermarried with members of surrounding nations who didn't worship Israel's God. That led them into idolatry. And that is why Ezra took such drastic measures in dealing with those who had intermarried with the heathen.

God demands that we keep separate from whatever defiles. This takes ruthless discipline. What is wrong must be utterly put away. What is right must be patiently and persistently developed. Separate yourself, therefore, to succeed.

6 MAY

"It is the Good News about his Son, Jesus Christ our Lord, who came as a human baby, born into King David's royal family line; and by being raised from the dead he was proved to be the mighty Son of God, with the holy nature of God Himself" (*Romans 1:3, 4, The Living Bible*).

Jesus Christ had a human ancestry through the line of David. He also had a divine nature which was eternal. Paul declares that His divine nature was proven through the resurrection. Thayer says, "For although Christ was the Son of God before His resurrection, yet He was openly appointed (*AV* declared) such among men by this transcendent and crowning event." Denney remarks, "The resurrection only declared Him to be what He truly was."

This demonstration or proof of Christ's deity was "in power," the power of God that raised our Lord from the dead, "according to the spirit of holiness" (*KJV*). This is not a reference to the Holy Spirit but to the spirit of Christ; that is, His divine nature. The characteristic quality of this divine nature is holiness. Jesus Christ is declared to be the Holy Son of God.

7 MAY

"Pilate . . . had decided to release Him. But you disowned the Holy and Righteous One" (*Acts 3:13, 14*).

Jesus Christ manifests His holiness by His attitude toward right and wrong. "You love right and hate wrong; so God, even your God, has poured out more gladness upon you than on anyone else" (*Hebrews 1:9, The Living Bible*).

There are those who crusade fervently against iniquity, with a holy hatred for sin, but do not have the same intensity of concern to *love righteousness*. Then there are others who feel very strongly about righteousness, but when there is a need to denounce evil they are silent. Jesus Christ did both. He loved righteousness, but when evil was being practiced in His presence He denounced it. In His conduct He never committed sin but always concerned Himself with doing that which pleased His heavenly Father. He loved right and hated wrong in perfect balance. May we follow His example.

8 MAY

PUTTING FEET TO YOUR PRAYERS—
NEHEMIAH (four days to read)
"But we prayed to our God, and because of them we set up a guard against them day and night" (Nehemiah 4:9).

A true man of prayer puts feet to his prayers. He is one who has learned that God doesn't do for us what He has already given us the ability to do for ourselves. God looks for people who pray about their work for Him. But He also looks for people who having prayed do His work.

God found such a man in Nehemiah. Obstacles and opposition from within and without were overcome by this man of prayer. With wisdom, winsomeness, and hard, sacrificial, down-to-earth work he led the people of God on to success. When the job was done, he gave God the glory and dedicated it to God. What a man! And all because he sought and served his God diligently and devotedly.

Such a life takes discipline. Discipline in prayer, planning, prosecuting, and perseverance. Discipline in thought, word, and deed. When one's work is done, have discipline in dedicating it all to God and to His glory.

9 MAY

"For we do not have a high priest who cannot sympathize with our weaknesses, but one who has been tempted in all things as we are, yet without sin" (Hebrews 4:15).

When Jesus Christ became man, He was tempted in all things as we are. In that way He could sympathize with our weakness. He knows from firsthand experience what it is like to be tempted as we are. Yet He stands unique in that He remained victorious over sin. It can be said only of Him among all men, "yet without sin."

The temptations Jesus Christ faced actually were not

designed to see whether or not He would succumb and fall
into sin. They were permitted by God to prove that He
could not sin. They were permitted to prove that He was
God, the Holy One, who by His very nature would find it
impossible to sin.

The temptations of Jesus Christ could be likened to the
tests engineers use when a bridge they have constructed is
completed. When they send cars and trucks over the bridge,
they do not do so to see whether or not it will stand. They
test it in this way to demonstrate that it is strong enough to
stand under that amount of weight.

Praise God, we have a high priest to represent us and He
has proven to be "holy and blameless, unstained by sin,
undefiled by sinners" (*Hebrews 7:26, The Living Bible*).

10 MAY

*"He made Him who knew no sin to be sin on
our behalf, that we might become the
righteousness of God in Him"* (*2 Corinthians 5:21*).

How infinitely God hates sin! He has such a strong desire
to wipe sin out that He will do what to us would be
inconceivable. Christ is here presented as not knowing sin;
that is, not experientially knowing sin. Yet He was willing
to let His heavenly Father put our sin upon Him in such a
way that it was identified with Him as though it was His
own. He was made to be sin! Think of the anguish. Think
of the moral pain. Yes, that is what it takes to put away sin.
The innocent becoming guilty by choice, to take the guilty
one's place.

Jesus Christ loves men and hates sin. Men are sinners. He
died to separate men from sin. His holiness moved Him to
do this as much as His love. Think long on His holiness
and you will begin to understand His love.

11 MAY

*"The precious blood of Christ, as of a lamb
without blemish and without spot"*
(*1 Peter 1:19, KJV*).

This is one of the most precious pictures of Jesus Christ
in all of the Bible. He was referred to as the "holy
servant" (*Acts 4:27, The Living Bible*). Even the demons
called Him "the holy Son of God" (*Mark 1:24; Luke 4:34,
The Living Bible*). Judas Iscariot confessed, "I have sinned,
for I have betrayed an innocent man" (*Matthew 27:4, The
Living Bible*). Satan himself could not find anything in
Jesus Christ's life which he could use to his own evil advantage (*John 14:30*).

Jesus was perfect through and through. This is why His
sacrifice is so effectual. Old Testament sacrifices covered sin
for a time. "How much more will the blood of Christ, who
through the eternal Spirit offered Himself without blemish
to God, cleanse your conscience from dead works to serve
the living God" (*Hebrews 9:14*).

The Bible repeatedly declares through many expressions
and figures the conclusion that Jesus Christ is absolutely
holy and morally pure. This is why, when we get to glory,
our song will ever be, "Worthy is the Lamb that was slain
to receive power and riches and wisdom and might and
honor and glory and blessing" (*Revelation 5:12*).

12 MAY

DECISIONS! DECISIONS!—ESTHER
(three days to read)

*"Go, assemble all the Jews who are found in Susa, and fast for
me; do not eat or drink for three days, night or day. I and my
maidens also will fast in the same way. And thus I will go in to
the king, which is not according to the law; and if I perish, I
perish"* (*Esther 4:16*).

Most of us are very ordinary. Yet we can do what God calls us to do. As Canon Farrar wrote:

I am only one, but I am one.
I cannot do everything, but I can do something.
What I can do, I ought to do.
What I ought to do, by the grace of God, I will do.

Esther was the only Israelite in a position to save her people from the wicked plans of Haman. Her chances for doing so were slim. But the urgency of the cause gripped her. She became willing to take her stand even if it meant death.

Her historic words, "I will go . . . and if I perish, I perish," have become an inspiration to many men and women of God. And many, like Esther, have succeeded in their mission against all odds because they have taken their stand as Esther did, rather than submitting to and succumbing under the power of the enemy.

First choose whom you will serve. Then choose His will at all times and in all details as you serve.

13 MAY

"Do you not know that your body is a temple of the Holy Spirit who is in you, whom you have from God, and that you are not your own? For you have been bought with a price: therefore glorify God in your body" (1 Corinthians 6:19, 20).

We are commanded as Christians to glorify God in our bodies, which have been purchased and are now God's possession. God wants us to keep our bodies pure because He has made each of us a temple of the Holy Spirit. He dwells within us.

The Holy Spirit is a title with significance. If you take the word *spirit* alone it does not communicate the same significance; angels too are spirits, and Satan is a spirit. The word *holy* likewise does not adequately communicate the identity of this One, for there are holy angels. But when you put the name *Holy Spirit* together with the article *the*, you distinguish the One who is truly unique. *The Holy Spirit* refers to the third person of the Godhead. Though unseen as spirit, He reveals to us the things of Christ. As one who is holy, He is trustworthy in every respect. And He is the One who makes the presence of God a reality in our lives.

14 MAY

"But the Helper, the Holy Spirit, whom the Father will send in My name . . ." (John 14:26).

As you start each day, stop and reflect for a moment on the momentous truth that God, the Holy Spirit, dwells within you. His very name indicates His own holiness. And He desires to impart holiness to others (*1 Peter 1:2*).

How thoughtlessly many of us talk about Him. We often want to experience His mighty work within us and yet we give little consideration to how unworthy and unholy we are. When we pray for the Holy Spirit to work in our churches, do we concern ourselves with whether we are ready to experience what He might have for us? He wants to have fellowship with us (*2 Corinthians 13:14*). He is present to empower us for service (Acts 1:8). As we trust Him He will manifest His fruit through our lives (*Galatians 5:22, 23*).

Consciously worship Him and commit your day and way to Him. Then cooperate with Him in proving "what the will of God is, that which is good and acceptable and perfect" (*Romans 12:2*).

15 MAY

BREAKTHROUGH—JOB
(fifteen days to read)

"I had heard about you before, but now I have seen you, and I loathe myself and repent in dust and ashes" (Job 42:5, 6, The Living Bible).

Thresher, the atomic submarine, was destroyed by pressure from without. The sea water was exerting greater force than the bulkheads could withstand.

Job knew pressure from without and within as he struggled to break through to God. But the end result made the endurance worthwhile.

In his pursuit of God, Job first faced the *material* test as his possessions were stolen and destroyed. Then he went through the *tragedy* test when his children were killed in a freak accident. When Job stood firm, Satan intensified his attack by putting him through a *physical* test. Job still didn't waver. The relentless dialogue between Job and his friends developed into what might be called a *mental* test. And this finally led to the *spiritual* test in which Job desperately cried out in faith for a consciousness of God's presence. His words shattered all barriers and brought Job to the place where God could abundantly bless him.

Learn from Job that no matter what test you are facing, patience and faith will overcome the pressure, and God will become more real to you personally.

16 MAY

"Holy, Holy, Holy, is the Lord of hosts, the whole earth is full of His glory" (Isaiah 6:3).

There are those who feel that this threefold declaration of the holiness of God refers to God as triune. That is possible since there is a plural reference to God in verse 8, "Who will go for *us*?"

Jesus addressed His Father as *Holy Father* in His high
priestly prayer in John 17:11. The angel Gabriel announced
to Mary, "The Holy Spirit will come upon you, and the
power of the Most High will overshadow you; and for that
reason the *holy offspring* shall be called the Son of God"
(*Luke 1:35*). And the very name of the third person of the
Trinity, the Holy Spirit, identifies Him as Holy. The
Trinity is a symphony of holiness, with nothing of
defilement within. No wonder all heaven echoes His holy
praises.

Let us make known this most glorious truth: Our God is
holy. Let us join the Psalmist: "Exalt the Lord our holy
God! Bow low before his feet . . . . Exalt the Lord our God,
and worship at his holy mountain in Jerusalem, for he is
holy" (*Psalm 99:5, 9, The Living Bible*).

17 MAY

"I saw the Lord . . . Then I said, 'Woe is me,
for I am ruined! Because I am a man of unclean
lips' " (Isaiah 6:1, 5).

Worship is our highest work. It must never be entered
into without consideration of who God is. Much frivolity in
church worship would vanish if congregations were keenly
aware that God is holy and that they are in His august
presence. It is instructive to note that the holy seraphim
cover their faces and feet in His holy presence.

This is not to say warmth, joy, freedom, and enjoyment
are not to be a part of worship. The Psalmist explains, "In
Thy presence is fulness of joy; In Thy right hand there are
pleasures forever" (*Psalm 16:11*). Nevertheless, when we
catch a glimpse of His holy presence we will see ourselves as
unholy, undone, unworthy. When overwhelmed with this
dilemma we are actually in the best frame of mind to
worship, for we realize then that fellowship with God is a
privilege, an honor, and we should seek such times with

Him often. We will also realize our need for the Holy Spirit's ministry within to enable us to worship aright. This is worshiping God in spirit and in truth. And God seeks such to worship Him.

18 MAY

"Everyone who practices sin also practices lawlessness, and sin is lawlessness" (1 John 3:4).

The Larger Catechism says: "Sin is any want of conformity unto, or transgression of, any law of God given as a rule to the reasonable creature."

"There is much in the world that men call evil that is not sin. We speak of cyclones, floods, earthquakes, frosts, drought, as evil, but none of these are sin. Likewise we speak of evil beasts . . . but do not imply that they are sinful. Our definition limits sin to 'the reasonable creature.' Those who are destitute of the organs of sense cannot know what sensation is. Those born blind cannot comprehend what sight is. None but rational creatures can know what sin is. Since man is a rational creature he knows that when he does what he ought not to do, or omits to do what he ought to do, or is what he ought not to be, or is not what he ought to be, he is chargeable with sin."[17]

19 MAY

"All have sinned and fall short of the glory of God" (Romans 3:23).

Trench, in his book *Synonyms of the New Testament,*

17. *Henry C. Thiessen, Lectures in Systematic Theology (Grand Rapids: Eerdmans, © 1949), p. 242. Used by permission.*

treats the subject of sin extensively. He says that sin "may be regarded under an infinite number of aspects, and in all languages has been so regarded; and as the diagnosis of it belongs most of all to the Scriptures, nowhere else are we likely to find it contemplated on so many sides, set forth under such various images. It may be regarded as the missing of a mark or aim; the overpassing or transgressing of a line; the disobedience to a voice; the falling where one should have stood upright; ignorance of what one ought to have known; diminishing of that which should have been rendered in full measure; non-observance of a law; a discord in the harmonies of God's universe; and in other ways almost out of number."[18]

20 MAY

"You shall love the Lord your God with all your heart, and with all your soul, and with all your mind. This is the great and foremost commandment. And a second is like it, you shall love your neighbor as yourself. On these two commandments depend the whole Law and the Prophets" (Matthew 22:37-40).

Being creatures who have both a moral sense and a rational capacity, we are subject to the law of right. Hodge points out that this law is not (a) our reason, for then every man would be a law unto himself and then there can be no sense of guilt; (b) the moral order of the universe, for this is but an abstraction and can neither impose obligation nor inflict penalty; (c) regard for the happiness of the universe, for it is manifest that happiness is not necessarily synonymous with goodness; (d) our own happiness, for such a view makes expediency the rule of right and wrong; but (e) it is subjection to the rule of a rational Being, God, who

18. *Robert Trench, Synonyms of the New Testament (Grand Rapids: Eerdmans, © 1950), n.p. Used by permission.*

is infinite, eternal, and immutable in His perfections.

In writing about this rule of a rational Being, expressed in His law, Paul concludes, "So then, the law is holy, and the commandment is holy and righteous and good" (*Romans 7:12*).

21 MAY

"For the Son of Man is going to come in the glory of His Father with His angels; and will then recompense every man according to his deeds" (*Matthew 16:27*).

"Several specific elucidations concerning the relation between the law and sin must be added. In the first place, failure to do what the law enjoins is as much sin as doing what it forbids. There are sins of omission as well as of commission (*James 4:17*). In the second place, to fail in one point is to be guilty of the whole (*Galatians 3:10; James 2:10*). One needs to break but one of God's commandments, not all of them, to be guilty in His sight. In the third place, ignorance of a law does not excuse a man . . . Ignorance of the law lessens the penalty as to degree, but not as to duration.

"In the fourth place, ability to keep the law is not essential to make the non-fulfillment sin. Man's inability to fulfill the law is due to his own part in the sin of Adam, and is not an original condition. Since the law of God expresses the holiness of God as the only standard for the creature, ability to obey cannot be the measure of obligation or the test of sin.

"And in the fifth place, the feeling of guilt is not necessary to the fact of sin. Man's moral standard may be so low and his conscience may have been so often sinned against, that he has practically no sense of sin left. The feeling of guilt is not necessary to the fact of sin in man's life."[19]

19. *Op. cit., Thiessen, pp. 243, 244.*

22 MAY

"If I am doing the very thing I do not wish, I am no longer the one doing it, but sin which dwells in me" (Romans 7:20).

Sin is thought by many to be only an act or thought, something done. The Bible declares that sin is a principle or nature within all of us. We are sinners by nature. What we think and do is a result of what we are, not vice versa. A corrupt tree can bring forth nothing but corrupt fruit (*Matthew 7:17, 18*). "For from the heart come evil thoughts, murder, adultery, fornication, theft, lying and slander" (*Matthew 15:19, The Living Bible*). Behind the act of murder is hatred. Behind the act of adultery is lust (*Matthew 5:21, 22, 27, 28*).

Paul distinguishes between sin and sins, pointing out that acts of sin are an expression of the sinful nature (*Romans 7:8, 9*). One does not become a sinner as a result of sinning. He sins because he is a sinner by nature. David confessed, "Behold, I was brought forth in iniquity, and in sin my mother conceived me" (*Psalm 51:5*).

The more mature one becomes spiritually, the deeper is one's repentance concerning the nature of sin. More so even than repentance from the acts of sin occasioned by this sinful nature.

23 MAY

"There are . . . things which the Lord hates" (*Proverbs 6:16*).

The Lord manifests His holiness in many ways. One way is by punishing sinners. He doesn't punish only because of the good the punishment will bring to the sinner. He punishes because He hates sin. He is never passive in His hatred of sin. That hatred must manifest itself. Isaiah 53:6 says, "All of us like sheep have gone astray, each of us has turned to his own way; But the Lord has caused the iniquity of us all to fall on Him." A literal translation of the Hebrew would read "caused to strike upon Him."

Any view of sin's punishment which ignores the fact that it is an expression of God's holy hatred of sin is both unbiblical and dishonoring to God. Occasionally our indignation is triggered by some enormous iniquity. God's reaction to the smallest sin is infinitely greater than our reaction to the worst sins imaginable.

24 MAY

"And according to the Law, one may almost say, all things are cleansed with blood, and without shedding of blood there is no forgiveness" (Hebrews 9:22).

Forgiveness demands a satisfaction of the holy demands of God's character and law. The only valid satisfaction is the shedding of innocent blood. No one can approach God on any other basis than shed blood. Any doctrine of the atonement which emphasizes an objective or motive other than to cover sin from God's view is a false doctrine.

In the sacrifice which Jesus Christ made on the cross He did more than cover sin from the holy gaze of God. That is the uniqueness of His sacrifice. It provided forgiveness that is permanent. It also provided cleansing that is thorough. Whenever we confess our sins, God forgives and cleanses and remembers them no more. Praise His holy name.

25 MAY

"That He might present to Himself the church in all her glory, having no spot or wrinkle or any such thing; but that she should be holy and blameless" (Ephesians 5:27).

The glorious goal of the church is "that she should be holy and blameless." The basis for reaching this goal is that her Savior is holy and blameless and His work makes it possible for Christians, individually and corporately, to become more holy and blameless each passing day. In Jude's benediction we read, "Now to Him who is able to keep you from stumbling, and to make you stand in the presence of His glory blameless with great joy" (*Jude 24*).

It is not possible for you to arrive at a place where it is impossible for you to sin—that comes when we are in glory. But it is possible to live a life of holiness and blamelessness if you consistently avail yourself of the adequate provisions God has made.

The old nature in our body is always ready to reassert itself if we consent and yield. That's why it is possible for all of us from time to time to stumble and sin. But we don't have to. We can, by faith, live victoriously over sin if we continuously reckon ourselves to be dead unto sin but alive unto God in Christ Jesus. "Do not let sin control your puny body any longer; do not give in to its sinful desires. Do not let any part of your bodies become tools of wickedness, to be used for sinning; but give yourselves completely to God— every part of you—for you are back from death and you want to be tools in the hands of God" (*Romans 6:12, 13, The Living Bible*).

26 MAY

"Do you not know that a little leaven leavens the whole lump of dough?" (1 Corinthians 5:6).

The Word of God declares God to be holy. Every person who becomes a child of God through faith in Jesus Christ is indwelt by the Holy Spirit. His body is the temple of the Holy Spirit. Furthermore, he becomes a member of the Church, which corporately is also the temple of the Holy Spirit. As such it is to be characterized by holiness. Any

Christian who works counter to this will find God dealing with him severely (*1 Corinthians 3:16, 17*).

Paul develops this more fully in discussing what the church of Corinth is to do about a member who is guilty of gross immorality. He points out that the church is to take action and excommunicate such a one from their fellowship (*1 Corinthians 5:1-5*). If they don't, they will discover that a little leaven (leaven is consistently used in the Bible to symbolically illustrate the nature of sin) will leaven the whole lump.

Paul instructs the church, "Clean out the old leaven, that you may be a new lump, just as you are in fact unleavened. For Christ our Passover also has been sacrificed. Let us therefore celebrate the feast, not with old leaven nor with the leaven of malice and wickedness, but with the unleavened bread of sincerity and truth" (*1 Corinthians 5:7, 8*). Such action is not easy, but it is essential if the holy character of the church is to be preserved.

27 MAY

"Bear one another's burdens, and thus fulfill the law of Christ" (Galatians 6:2).

Jesus gives a detailed procedure for correcting an erring brother in the church. If you are aware of a brother in Christ sinning against you or merely sinning, before others become aware of it "go to him privately and confront him with his fault. If he listens and confesses it, you have won back a brother. But if not, then take one or two others with you and go back to him again, proving everything you say by these witnesses" (*Matthew 18:15, 16, The Living Bible*). According to Paul's letter to the Galatians (*6:1*), you and the ones you take with you are to be spiritual, mature Christians.

"If he still refuses to listen, then take your case to the church, and if the church's verdict favors you, but he won't

accept it, then the church should excommunicate him"
(*Matthew 18:17, The Living Bible*). This is essentially the
same kind of judgment as Paul talked about when he
instructed the Corinthians "to deliver such a one to Satan."

This process of counsel and discipline must always be
carried out with a spirit of love, humility, and "gentleness;
looking to yourself, lest you too be tempted" (*Galatians 6:1*).

28 MAY

*"If a brother sins against you, go to him
privately and confront him with his fault. If he
listens and confesses it, you have won back a brother"*
(*Matthew 18:15, The Living Bible*).

The focus here is on helping an erring brother *in private*.
If the sin is one which is known by only a few, the desired
procedure is to so deal with it that no more might get to
know about it. If the brother responds positively and is
restored to fellowship with God and to those who might
have been wronged, then no one else needs to know about it.

If the sin, however, is of a public nature, known
throughout the church and/or the community, then the
resolution of the problem must of necessity be of a public
nature. Had Peter shared with Paul his partial feelings
toward Gentile believers, Paul would have reproved him in
private. But since Peter's attitude resulted in action which
was public, Paul dealt with him in a public form (*Galatians
2:11-17*; note especially verse 14).

Love prompted this action. Love, not just for Peter, but
for all affected by his action. Paul wanted Peter to have the
wholesome effect upon all present which the gospel affords.
Love doesn't take the easy road. Love does what is necessary,
even if initially it hurts. Love is always careful.

29 MAY

"These men are those who are hidden reefs [stains] in your love-feasts when they feast with you without fear, caring for themselves" (*Jude 12*).

Jude and Peter (*2 Peter 2:13*) both express the indictment of God upon those who as false teachers infiltrate local churches to lead others astray while they gratify their own selfish desires. Their activities are especially evil when they arrogantly participate in the love-feast, which was a common meal associated with the Lord's Supper.

Paul focused on the same wanton attitude evident in the Corinthian church (*1 Corinthians 11:20-34*). Fellowship around the Lord's Supper is to be characterized by love and holiness. We are encouraged to examine ourselves so that we don't partake of the elements unworthily. It is the responsibility of the leader in the church to remind fellow believers of this. He should also make it very clear that to partake of the Lord's Supper as an unbeliever is sheer hypocrisy. He should warn of God's judgment on those who knowingly take this matter lightly. The Lord's Supper is to be a holy communion with God and with fellow believers.

30 MAY

BLESSEDNESS—PSALMS (forty days to read)
"For Jehovah God is our Light and our Protector. He gives us grace and glory. No good thing will he withhold from those who walk along his paths. O Lord of the armies of heaven, blessed are those who trust in you" (*Psalm 84:11, 12, The Living Bible*).

The Psalms show us that life has its valleys as well as its mountaintop experiences, its dark and dreary days as well as bright ones. According to F. B. Meyer, a spiritual giant of the nineteenth century, "certain fruits of the Christian life such as meekness, gentleness, kindness, and humility cannot come to perfection if the sun of prosperity always shines." You can know true blessedness—the awareness of God's favor—no matter what your circumstances in life if you follow the directives of the book of Psalms.

The opening words of Psalm 1 give the first directive: study the Bible. The Bible explains our need for salvation. Sin is the root problem, so confess it and trust God to forgive. Stability in your faith and sharing it with others are two further directives which bring blessing. The book of Psalms also emphasizes prayer and praise.

Go to God's Word, believe what it says, live by it, and share it, never forgetting to thank God for all He reveals and promises to you. Oh, the blessedness of such a life!

31 MAY

"How can a young man keep his way pure? By keeping it according to Thy word" (Psalm 119:9).

Bible reading, study, memorization, and meditation are essential ingredients of a holy life. A faithful servant of God has said, "The more of God's Word I master, the harder it is for me to sin. Before any temptation to sin has become very strong, the Holy Spirit floods my mind with numerous Bible truths both as to why I should not yield and how I might overcome the temptation." This is why the Psalmist declared the blessedness of the person whose "delight is in the law of the Lord, and in His law he meditates day and night" (*Psalm 1:2*).

Anyone can keep his way pure by learning the Word of God and then obeying it. The Psalmist testifies, "Thy Word have I treasured [hid] in my heart, that I may not sin against Thee" (Psalm 119:11). The Word of God in the heart is the great protector against going into sin. It is "a lamp to my feet, and a light to my path" (Psalm 119:105).

1 JUNE

"Great is our Lord, and abundant in strength;
His understanding is infinite" (Psalm 147:5).

God's understanding is infinite because His knowledge is perfect (*Job 37:16*). The apostle John said that God "knows everything we do" (*1 John 3:20*), *The Living Bible*). There is nothing God does not know perfectly. He is omniscient.

There are no afterthoughts with God. He is never in a position where He doesn't know both every possibility as well as the right one among the many. He is never cornered. He always has the right answer, though in His wisdom He does not always share the answer with us.

God never needs counsel from anyone, nor can anyone instruct Him (*Romans 11:33, 34*). "No one can fathom the depths of his understanding" (*Isaiah 40:28*), *The Living Bible*). When we go to God in prayer, we are not informing Him about our need. He knows our need. He also knows how to meet our need and when best to meet it. Prayer is finding comfort and confidence through communion with the One who understands perfectly, and then by faith taking hold of His willingness to help.

2 JUNE

"Are not two sparrows sold for a cent? And yet
not one of them will fall to the ground apart
from your Father" (Matthew 10:29).

The astounding thing about the omniscience of God is His knowledge of the smallest detail. He knows how many stars are in the vast heavens. In fact, He has a name for each one (*Psalm 147:4*). He also knows the number of hairs you have on your head (*Matthew 10:30*). All the sparrows, though they are among the smaller birds, are individually known by God. He knows when anything happens to one of them.

All that is in the vast universe He has created is known to Him. All, even to the most minute microcosm, is clear in His mind. God knows your human frailty, that you are but dust (*Psalm 103:14*). He knows your circumstances. He is fully aware of the pressures you are facing. When perplexed by what you are experiencing, one thing you can be certain of: God knows, and has promised never to let you be tempted beyond what you are able to endure (*1 Corinthians 10:13*).

3 JUNE

"Thou dost know when I sit down and when I rise up; Thou dost understand my thought from afar" (*Psalm 139:2*).

The Psalmist expresses an awareness of how thoroughly God knows him and declares: "Even before there is a word on my tongue, behold, O Lord, Thou dost know it all. Such knowledge is too wonderful for me; it is too high, I cannot attain to it" (*Psalm 139:4, 6*). I have often had to ask someone to repeat what he has said because it has not been clear. God never needs to have us repeat ourselves. The tongue is prompted to say what the mind formulates and dictates. God knows what we are going to say because He understands our thoughts even at a distance. That includes more than the deliberate thoughts when we are formulating ideas in relation to a certain project. He understands even the imaginations that flit through our minds (1 Chronicles 28:9).

That's why Jesus emphasized the importance of not only our actions, but also our attitudes and affections (Matthew 5:27, 28). You might fool all people some of the time, and some people all the time, but you never fool God.

4 JUNE

*"I am God, and there is no one like Me,
declaring the end from the beginning and from
ancient times things which have not been done"*
(Isaiah 46:9, 10).

Being omniscient, God knows everything thoroughly in
the eternal present. He knows what happened in past
eternities as clearly as if they were happening now. He also
knows everything that will happen throughout future
millennia as if they were taking place right now. Nothing is
uncertain to Him! There are no surprises for Him.

God knows who will respond to the gospel and He
knows what it will take for those who will respond to do so.
In His wisdom, He chooses those whom He will to become
His children *(Ephesians 1:9, 12).* He does this, however,
without violating the free will of man *(Romans 10:13).* To
our finite minds this has the appearance of contradiction.
But the wisdom of God declares them to be complementary
and harmonious. Dr. J. I. Packer calls this an antinomy:
two complementary truths which have the appearance of
contradiction.

5 JUNE

*"In whom are hidden all the treasures of
wisdom and knowledge" (Colossians 2:3).*

It might not always be evident in studying the life of
Jesus Christ that He is omniscient. But He possesses all the
treasures of wisdom and knowledge. It is just that they are
possessed in a hidden way. Anyone who seeks after the
Savior and follows Him discovers that He knows all things
and is able to counsel and guide with wisdom.

The important word in this verse is *all.* There is nothing
He does not know. And more, He has all wisdom so that

He is able to apply His infinite knowledge in the best way to your particular need.

Jesus Christ knew what His earthly life was going to be like. He knew His own would reject Him. He knew He would be condemned unjustly by men. He knew He would be crucified. He knew the agony it would be to bear the sin of man and have His Father forsake Him while He made that ultimate saving sacrifice. He knew and was still willing to go through with it, because He loved. Praise His holy name.

6 JUNE

"But Jesus, on His part, was not entrusting Himself to them, for He knew all men, and because He did not need any one to bear witness concerning man for He Himself knew what was in man" (John 2:24, 25).

Jesus Christ knows you through and through. He knows all about all men. It is obvious that Jesus knew the secret history of the woman at the well *(John 4:16-19)*. He knows all about your past too. When He was in circumstances where men didn't agree with what He was doing, He knew their thoughts *(Mark 2:8)*. You can't rationalize in an argument with Jesus Christ without His being aware of your very thought patterns. It is interesting to note that Jeremiah declared, "The heart is the most deceitful thing there is, and desperately wicked. No one can really know how bad it is. Only the Lord knows! He searches all hearts and examines deepest motives so he can give to each person his right reward, according to his deeds—how he has lived" *(Jeremiah 17:9, 10, The Living Bible)*. Since Jesus knows the heart of man, He must be God.

According to John 6:64 Jesus had foreknowledge, for He knew from the beginning who was an unbeliever and that Judas would be His betrayer. Jesus was not surprised at the actions and accusations of Judas. As you read the Gospel narratives it is obvious that Jesus knew not just what God was going to do, but also what certain men and even a certain fish would do (*Matthew 17:27*).

7 JUNE

"And another time when he appeared to them, they asked him, 'Lord, are you going to free Israel [from Rome] now and restore us as an independent nation?' 'The Father sets those dates,' he replied, 'and they are not for you to know' " (Acts 1:6, 7, The Living Bible).

Jesus Christ is omniscient. However, when He became a man He emptied Himself of the independent exercise of His divine attributes. He had understanding and insight into most things. But, for example, He told His disciples that only God the Father knew the time of His return to establish His Kingdom.

This is why Jesus Christ spent long hours of the night in prayer before He chose His disciples (*Luke 6:12, 13*). He also spent extended hours in prayer before dawn to seek His Father's will concerning the conduct of His mission (*Mark 1:35-38*). It is a beautiful picture of the humility of Jesus Christ, our great example.

8 JUNE

"Although He was a Son, He learned obedience from the things which He suffered" (*Hebrews 5:8*).

The translation should read, "Though He was Son by nature." Christ's deity is being emphasized here. The idea is,

"Though He was the Son of God, God the Son, Very God of Very God, yet He learned obedience by the things He suffered." As God, he knew what obedience was. But only after becoming man could He experience it. As God He had no one to whom He owed obedience. But when He assumed a human body He also assumed a position in which He now obeyed His heavenly Father. In practicing obedience He learned experientially what it was.

It should be noted that Jesus Christ always did those things that pleased the Father (*John 8:29*). His obedience was an extension of that into His human experience. Vincent says that "He required the special discipline of a severe human experience as a training for His office as a high priest who could be touched with the feeling of human infirmities. He did not need to be disciplined out of any inclination to disobedience." Alford says: "The special course of submission by which He became perfected as our high priest was gone through in time, and was a matter of acquirement and practice." Jesus grew in wisdom also (*Luke 2:52*). The only learning or growing one who is perfect can do is in the laboratory of experience.

9 JUNE

"Who has directed the Spirit of the Lord, or as His counselor has informed Him?"
(*Isaiah 40:13*).

The Holy Spirit is presented by Isaiah as being omniscient. No one can teach Him anything, not even the Father or the Son. He searches the deep things of God and knows them thoroughly. He knows the will of God perfectly. He knows you and your circumstances and what is needed to work out God's will in your life. He has been sent to instruct you in the truth of God. Jesus promised, "He will guide you into all the truth" (*John 16:13*).

When Jesus said that the Holy Spirit would teach you only what He was told to teach you, He was not inferring that the Holy Spirit was unable to teach anything else. He simply meant that in the economy of God, the Holy Spirit agreed to submit Himself to the directives of the Father and the Son. In this He exemplified genuine humility and the harmony of the Trinity.

10 JUNE

"Why has Satan filled your heart to lie to the Holy Spirit?" (Acts 5:3).

The Holy Spirit, as spirit, is able to penetrate our beings and probe into the very innermost thoughts and intents of our hearts and minds. Satan too, as a spirit being, has access to our thought life. He can know what you are thinking. He can analyze your thought patterns to determine how you will respond to certain stimuli. And then he is crafty in devising temptations tailor-made to strike at your vulnerable areas. He knows what will be the most deadly attack.

Being able to produce a desired effect upon all men, he is able to mastermind and orchestrate circumstances in such a way that his evil designs for the world are quite successful. As the prince of this world, he has significant influence on the way things turn out. But it should be remembered, he is limited in his knowledge. He can deceive us, but he cannot deceive God. God has set boundaries beyond which Satan cannot go.

11 JUNE

"And the great dragon was thrown down, the serpent of old who is called the Devil and Satan, who deceives the whole world; he was thrown down

to the earth, and his angels were thrown down with him"
(Revelation 12:9).

Satan, with his access to the minds of men, can do a
fantastic job of deception. He is the one behind the
phenomenon of spiritism. He helps mediums know things
about others by relating to them what he knows about
them. When a medium supposedly communicates with the
dead, it is simply a matter of Satan or Satan's demons
transferring information and impressions.

When it comes to predicting events in the future, Satan
can do so with a measure of accuracy because he knows
what people are thinking and planning as future activities.
Satan knows, for example, if someone is planning to hurt
someone else. He also knows what others are planning for
the same place and time period. He can then evaluate the
possibilities of the evil deed being carried out. And then he
can communicate this to a medium. A percentage of
accuracy can be maintained this way. What Satan knows
about the future, however, is limited. He does not have the
ability to know the future as God does. This is one of the
reasons why God ultimately will triumph over Satan.

12 JUNE

*"The god of this world has blinded the minds
of the unbelieving" (2 Corinthians 4:4).*

There is a two-fold reason why the natural man cannot
understand the things of God. First: through the fall, sin
has rendered man spiritually dead and unable to
comprehend spiritual truth. To the person who is dead in
sin, spiritual truth is often foolishness.

Second: when God exposes such a person to "the light of
the gospel of the glory of Christ," Satan begins his work of
blinding that person's eyes to the truth *(2 Corinthians 4:4)*.
Paul indicates that Satan does this by veiling the truth from
the view of the unbeliever *(2 Corinthians 4:3)*. Satan is the

great distracter, suggesting all kinds of deviating ideas to the mind of the seeker after truth, trying to blind him or distract him for meditation and application. Satan knows that when anyone comes to know the truth, he is by that truth set free from the lies and deceptions of the kingdom of darkness.

A Christian is challenged no longer to walk as the nonbelievers who are "blinded and confused. Their closed hearts are full of darkness; they are far away from the life of God because they have shut their minds against him, and they cannot understand his ways" (*Ephesians 4:17, 18, The Living Bible*).

13 JUNE

"For now we see in a mirror dimly, but then face to face; now I know in part, but then I shall know fully just as I also have been fully known" (*1 Corinthians 13:12*).

Man was created in the image of God. This likeness to God included his ability to know, to think. Man has the capacity to observe, evaluate, relate ideas, think, and know things. He has made fantastic strides in acquiring knowledge. In the realm of science, knowledge is exploding. Yet the most knowledgeable are usually ready to acknowledge that man at best is just scratching the surface of what is knowable.

How often we think or say, "If only I had known . . ." That is our problem: we know only in part. This is true of our daily experience. Every problem we tackle, every decision we make, every plan we develop, every judgment we make is based on partial knowledge.

Psychologists say that we use only a small percentage of our brain potential. But even if we were to think at 100% performance, we still would not know thoroughly. We are finite creatures. We have limits beyond which we can't go. A day is coming when we will know in a way far beyond our earthly limits, but until that day we must depend upon the wisdom of God for the ultimate answers to life.

14 JUNE

"The knowledge of the Holy One is understanding" (Proverbs 9:10).

Though man sees or knows only as though he were looking through a darkened glass, it is possible for him to know what is necessary for his life to be full and meaningful. He can know the Holy One, God. In a general way he comes to this knowledge first through natural revelation. Seeing the vastness, beauty, and order of the universe around them, men can't help but see God's "invisible attributes, His eternal power and divine nature . . . being understood through what has been made, so that they are without excuse" *(Romans 1:20).*

To know God personally you must read or hear God's revelation of Himself as recorded in the Bible. In the Bible you discover the personality and love of God. It is there you see Him in His Triune glory. The Holy Spirit has taken the deep things of God and guided holy men to record these truths in an unerring way. Then the Holy Spirit illumines the believer's heart and mind to understand so that he can really know. The prophet said, "Then shall we know, if we follow on to know the Lord" *(Hosea 6:3, KJV).*

15 JUNE

"I have more insight than all my teachers, for Thy testimonies are my meditation" (Psalm 119:99).

It is in the Bible that man finds the ultimate questions of life answered. God knows our needs and our concerns about them. He knows how to meet those needs and has recorded His solutions. If we follow the instructions carefully we will discover God's answer experientially.

Too often we "walk in the counsel of the wicked . . . stand in the path of sinners . . . sit in the seat of scoffers."

The Psalmist declares, "How blessed is the man . . . [whose] delight is in the law of the Lord, and in His law he meditates day and night" *(Psalm 1:1, 2)*. Such a student of the Word of God will indeed have more insight than his worldly teachers. He will be able to say with the psalmist, "[Your words] make me wiser than my enemies . . . . They make me even wiser than the aged" (P*salm 119:98, 100*), *The Living Bible*).

There are some things we can never discover purely by observation. They must be revealed. God has graciously revealed all we need to know to enter, establish, and maintain our saving relationship with Him.

16 JUNE

"Grow in the grace and knowledge of our Lord and Savior Jesus Christ" (2 Peter 3:18).

We are exhorted to grow in grace. But grace is what God does for us. We cannot produce grace or even add to it. We can only accept the grace of God and allow it to operate in us. This takes place as a direct result of our knowledge of Jesus Christ, and in proportion to how well we know Him. The better we know Him, the easier it is for us to accept, expect, and allow Him to work in us.

It is also true that we increase in our knowledge of God as a result of obeying Him *(Colossians 1:10)*. If in obeying God I find myself in difficulties beyond my control and then find God working them out and delivering me, I will increase in my knowledge of His faithfulness. I might formerly have had a head knowledge of His faithfulness. Now I know experientially.

17 JUNE

"But of that day and hour no one knows, not even the angels of heaven" (Matthew 24:36).

It might be assumed that because the angels are in the presence of God, worshiping Him, serving Him, watching Him, that they would be aware of what God is doing and planning. They evidently have a greater knowledge of things than man does, but it is limited.

One matter that they have a hard time fully comprehending is man's salvation. They know when someone becomes a child of God and they rejoice over each one who is added to the ranks of the redeemed (*Luke 15:10*); yet they don't understand the meaning of the salvation experience and the new relationship with God that a lost, sinful man can know through Christ. They are curious about this; they want to look into it (*1 Peter 1:12*).

There are indications in the Bible that each of us has a guardian angel. To watch over and care for a person, a guardian angel must know what confronts us day by day, and must work out a strategy for our protection.

18 JUNE

"And as for you, the anointing which you received from Him abides in you, and you have no need for any one to teach you; but as His anointing teaches you about all things, and is true and is not a lie, and just as it has taught you, you abide in Him" (1 John 2:27).

The anointing which John here refers to is a work of the Holy Spirit by which He teaches us. Every Christian is

indwelt by the Holy Spirit (*Romans 8:9*). Every Christian
has this great, infinitely wise teacher as a permanent
resident in his life. At any time he can call on the Holy
Spirit for guidance in understanding the truth as found in
the Bible. Jesus Christ promised, "But when He, the Spirit
of truth, comes, He will guide you into all the truth; for He
will not speak on His own initiative, but whatever He
hears, He will speak; and He will disclose to you what is to
come" (*John 16:13*).

In an important sense no believer should be dependent on
others for his growth in spiritual understanding. Any
believer can go to God's Word and independently learn
what God has said. Too many Christians wait upon others
to spoon-feed them or give them a spiritual shot in the arm.
If left to themselves, they would soon shrivel up and
deteriorate into worthless branches (*John 15:6*). Most Sunday
Christians fall into this category. To such persons the writer
of Hebrews declares, "You have been Christians a long time
now, and you ought to be teaching others, but instead you
have dropped back to the place where you need someone to
teach you all over again the very first principles in God's
Word. You are like babies who can drink only milk, not old
enough for solid food" (*Hebrews 5:12, The Living Bible*).

19 JUNE

*"And God has appointed in the church . . .
teachers"* (*1 Corinthians 12:28*).

We have seen that with the anointing of the Holy Spirit,
we are not dependent on a teacher to give us our
understanding of the Word of God. However, we must not
ignore the teaching in the Bible that God has appointed
some whom He has chosen and gifted to be teachers in the
church. In other words, members of the church do need to
be taught. We rob ourselves if we neglect the assembling of
ourselves together as the manner of some is (*Hebrews 10:25*).
We need to experience the unique ministry of teachers who,
guided by the Holy Spirit, are able to show us the deep

things of God. Pastors are to be teachers; the final gift to the church mentioned in Ephesians 4:11 is the pastor-teacher.

The double thrust is that we are to learn from the teaching of those God has appointed as teachers in the church, and also from our own personal, prayerful Bible study. We should be like the Bereans who listened to those who taught in public and then went home for personal study to see whether what was said was indeed biblical (*Acts 17:11*).

20 JUNE

"For to one is given the word of wisdom through the Spirit" (1 Corinthians 12:8).

This gift, the word of wisdom, is the ability to comprehend deeply the mysteries of God. It goes beyond the natural ability to see and hear. A person with this gift has a unique ability to find spiritual gems in the simplest phrase of Scripture. Then having found the gem of truth, this one is able to relate it to life so that it can be readily applied to individual situations. A simple definition of this gift is "the application of spiritual truth." All believers are to have wisdom (*Colossians 1:9; James 1:5*). Some with the *gift* of wisdom, however, are able to assist the other members of the body by clarifying and crystallizing the truth, and by putting it into a form easy to apply.

21 JUNE

"To another [is given] the word of knowledge according to the same Spirit" (*1 Corinthians 12:8*).

The gift of knowledge differs from the gift of wisdom in that it focuses on just the facts. One with this gift is generally thought of as a scholar. He finds delight in research, digging for the facts. He might spend a lifetime studying ancient scrolls or manuscripts. He might be involved in archaeological expeditions. Or he might seek answers to thorny problems of theology. Many would find this dry and discouraging, but all of us benefit from the discovery of facts which substantiate the Word of God and help us better understand the meaning of words and contexts.

We must be careful not to relegate all research and study to those with this gift. We are all encouraged to study in order to show ourselves approved of God, workmen who don't need to be ashamed (*2 Timothy 2:15*). All believers are the recipients of wisdom and knowledge (*1 Corinthians 1:5, 30*); yet we will benefit greatly if we recognize those specially gifted in these areas and let them minister to us.

22 JUNE

"To another [is given] the distinguishing of spirits" (*1 Corinthians 12:10*).

The gift of distinguishing or discernment of spirits was given by God to protect the church from false teachers and their doctrine. Certain members of the body are able to determine who is right and who is wrong, that is, whether they are of God or of Satan. Satan often tries to deceive the church by coming into their midst as an angel of light or directing an available human being to function as though he were a true messenger of God while teaching error. Often the way he does this is by counterfeiting the gifts of the Spirit of God. To recognize this is more than natural insight or discernment.

Peter used this gift when he asked Ananias, "Why has Satan filled your heart to lie to the Holy Spirit?" (*Acts 5:3*). How did he know? He knew because he had this gift of discernment. Every Christian is taught in the Bible,

"Beloved, do not believe every spirit, but test the spirits to see whether they are from God; because many false prophets have gone out into the world" (*1 John 4:1*).

23 JUNE

"Knowledge will increase" (Daniel 12:4).

Daniel was specially gifted of God to foretell significant events in the plan of God for the ages. His prophecies become a framework for understanding other prophecies. At the close of his most important work, God informs him that in the end times knowledge will increase.

The increase of knowledge is quite natural, of course, since we can always build upon what others have discovered, and can spare ourselves repetition of others' mistakes. But the knowledge explosion in recent decades is nothing short of phenomenal.

There's always the danger that we begin to feel we are self-sufficient, and that we don't need God. And as knowledge increases, the "we can make it on our own" fallacy becomes yet greater. Such reasoning very likely is a major factor in man's ultimate downfall—and in the need for God's judgment in the end.

There is a sense, however, in which the increase of knowledge can be a boon to us. There is more we can learn about God, His works, His Word. In a unique way, this is a part of the preparation whereby we become better prepared to meet Him.

24 JUNE

"God will send upon them a deluding influence so that they might believe what is false" (*2 Thessalonians 2:11*).

Yes, knowledge will increase in the end times. But the sad fact is that many will reject the truth they know, and will arrogantly follow the father of lies and deception, even Satan. Because of their rebellion, God will further intensify their plight by sending upon them a deluding influence to believe what is false.

This fact alone should sober us to the harsh reality of how a heart is spiritually hardened. The wise man said, "A man who hardens his neck after much reproof will suddenly be broken beyond remedy" (*Proverbs 29:1*). If we are right with God and responsive to Him, then we should also be concerned about others who are resisting the truth. We should do all we can to get them to respond positively to the truth of God. "Dear brothers, if anyone has slipped away from God and no longer trusts the Lord, and someone helps him understand the Truth again, that person who brings him back to God will have saved a wandering soul from death, bringing about the forgiveness of his many sins" (*James 5:19, 20, The Living Bible*).

25 JUNE

"We proclaim Him [Jesus Christ], admonishing every man and teaching every man with all wisdom, that we may present every man complete in Christ" (*Colossians 1:28*).

There is a real need to reemphasize the importance of teaching when we proclaim Christ to the world. When we call sinners to put their faith in Jesus Christ for salvation, we should be sure they know what they are doing. There is danger in getting people to make premature responses. Jesus never made it easy for people to respond to His salvation. Sometimes it seems as though He put people off. Once he even suggested to the disciples that they consider leaving Him, as others had done.

We should teach every man, or at least try to. And we should teach with all wisdom. That means we should be well prepared, thoroughly versed in the truth of the Bible, so as to give an answer to every man who asks us a reason of the hope we have (*1 Peter 3:15*). We should also seek to understand the views others hold, so that we can give appropriate explanations of the truth and relate it in a meaningful way to their views. We must be careful, also, to be uncompromising. The goal of presenting every man mature in Christ will keep us on course as we work with those who seek the truth.

26 JUNE

"But if any of you lacks wisdom, let him ask of God, who gives to all men generously and without reproach, and it will be given to him" (James 1:5).

Circumstances often perplex us. We wonder why God allows certain things to come our way. We might even wonder if continuing to go on with Christ is really worth it all. At such times we need wisdom from above.

Wisdom from above comes in a number of ways. Studying God's Word will expose us to His wisdom and give us guidelines to follow. Seeking the counsel of mature Christians who have learned from experience is also helpful. Or, as suggested in this portion of James, we should "ask of God." This demands honesty and humility to admit we have a lack of wisdom. From this position of lack, we must recognize and acknowledge God's infinite supply of wisdom. Also, we must acknowledge His gracious willingness to share His wisdom freely. Then by faith we must ask for it without wavering, expecting God to give it generously. Finally by faith we must use the wisdom God gives, fearlessly and faithfully. That's the way to endure patiently the tests of our faith so that the perfecting process might operate in our lives until ultimately we are mature and "complete, lacking in nothing" (*James 1:2-4*).

27 JUNE

"All Scripture is inspired by God" (2 Timothy 3:16).

In church history you can find three main views of authority. Some believe that the Church is the prime source of authority. When issues arise they turn to the Church's traditions and present teachings, and say, "I believe as I do because that's the position my church takes." Others believe that reason is our final authority. "I believe thus and so because it seems to me to be the most reasonable answer." The third view is that the Bible, God's Word, is where authority ultimately resides. "I believe thus and so because God says it is so in His Word." This third view is the evangelical view of authority.

Why? Because the first two views, tradition and reason, are merely the words and ideas of humans. Though important for reference, those sources must occupy only a subordinate place to the Word, which is God-breathed. Though men were the instruments used in recording what is in the Bible, it was the Holy Spirit who guided them in recording only what God wanted. Tradition and reason are relative. God's Word is certain. It is our primary and supreme authority.

28 JUNE

"For no prophecy was ever made by an act of human will, but men moved by the Holy Spirit spoke from God" (2 Peter 1:21).

The word "moved" is a participle which could be translated "when moved." Further, it is in the passive voice, which indicates "to be moved upon." This means that men did not initiate the writing of the Scriptures. They wrote when moved to do so by the Holy Spirit. And as they wrote, the Holy Spirit moved upon them, guiding them in expression and superintending the recording so that it would be not only accurate but clear to the careful reader.

This work of the Holy Spirit also included the work of imparting truth to the writers which they did not previously know or which they could come to know in no other way. In this "moving upon" the writers, however, the Holy Spirit did not violate their individual style of communication. He did not dictate every word and indicate every matter of sentence structure. Instead He saw to it that what was recorded was an accurate presentation of the truth.

29 JUNE

"Men moved by the Holy Spirit spoke from God" (2 Peter 1:21).

We must understand that the process of inspiration operated in persons, not machines. This is obvious from the different literary styles. God sovereignly worked in selecting men for this task. He also influenced their lives by the family environment in which they grew up. Then He allowed circumstances to develop within which character was built, lessons were learned, messages were born. Finally He brought it all together so that each one's ministry was in harmony with his life and experience.

It is no accident that Moses, who grew up in Pharaoh's house, was to become the great lawgiver. Likewise, it was no accident that the justice of God was declared by Amos, the love of God by Hosea, and the sovereignty of God by Isaiah. Paul became the apostle of God's grace and the life of faith. James proclaimed the importance of works. John the beloved emphasized the message of love. All were moved upon by the Holy Spirit, not only for the specific task of writing, but throughout their lives in preparation for the writing.

30 JUNE

"All Scripture is inspired by God" (2 Timothy 3:16).

The word "inspired" literally means "God-breathed." When a bass and a tenor sing, each sounds different. What makes their sound to be different? When we speak, air passes over our vocal cords to produce the sound. Essentially the same air is used to produce differing sounds. A bass singer's vocal cords differ from a tenor's not in kind but in degree—that's what makes their voices sound different. Similarly, the holy men of old who wrote the Scriptures were all different in various degrees. As the breath of God flowed through them, they sounded different.

Some were fiery extroverts. Others were melancholy introverts. Some were scholars with well-trained, logical minds. Others were uneducated farmers or fishermen. What made them one was the "breath of God" which flowed through them in inspiration. That breath was the origin of their message.

1 JULY

"God is love" (1 John 4:8).

It is commonly stated that what the world
needs is love. One of the most basic needs each of us has is
the need to be loved. Yet in our materialistic world it is easy
to become unaware of this dimension of life. Christianity
presents to the world the only true, dependable love
available to humanity. That love is the love of God.

God is unique in that there is never a thought in His
mind out of harmony with His love. There is never an act
of God performed out of harmony with His love. He always
thinks, acts, and responds in a way that corresponds to His
love.

None of His attributes, such as justice or holiness,
contradict His attribute of love. Nor does the fact that He is
love cause Him to overlook sin or ignore the need to punish
sin. God ever was, is, and ever will be love.

2 JULY

"God is love" (1 John 4:8).

It is helpful to expound this statement
further. Some might think that since God is love it would
be correct to say that love is God. Dr. Wuest exposes the
fallacy of such reasoning. "As to the statement, 'God is
love,' we would suggest that that simply is not true. God is
not an abstraction. The word 'God' has the article, the word
'love' does not, which construction in Greek means that the
two words are not interchangeable. The absence of the
article emphasizes nature, essence, character. The translation
should read, 'God as to His nature is love.' That is, God is
a loving God. It is His nature to be loving."[20]

W. E. Vine says, "In respect of [the word] *agapao* as used of God, it expresses the deep and constant love and interest of a perfect Being towards entirely unworthy objects."[21]

3 JULY

"Beloved, let us love one another, for love is from God" (1 John 4:7).

It is proper to say that no one can love as he ought to love until He knows God and allows God to be in control of his life. You can muster emotion, feeling, empathy, concern, but not true love. Love is from God, not from man.

One kind of love man manifests is *erotic* love. This is the sexual feeling that arises within the being of even sinful persons. It is selfish, self-satisfying. It is concerned with what one can get, rather than what one can give. It is nothing like God's love.

Another kind of love is *phileo*, or tender affection. This is a love prompted by the desirable qualities found in the person loved. It is based on the fact of likeness or familiarity to oneself. It is akin to liking or finding pleasure in something. It involves affection or fondness and is a purely human attachment to another. This is a legitimate, wholesome kind of love, but is never used when God commands us to the life of love. If you have never reached beyond this level of loving you don't know what you have been missing.

20. *Op. cit., Wuest, In These Last Days, pp. 163, 164.*
21. *Op. cit., Vine, Vol. 3, p. 21.*

4 JULY

*"But that the world may know that
I love the Father, and as the Father gave Me
commandment, even so I do" (John 14:31).*

Above all else Jesus wanted the world to know that He
loved the Father. Loving the Father was the secret of His
life. If you would like to show love to the heavenly Father,
make a study of how Jesus did this in His life on earth—
then follow His example.

Jesus taught that the first and great commandment is,
"You shall love the Lord your God with all your heart,
and with all your soul, and with all your mind" (*Matthew
22:37, 38*). He supremely demonstrated obedience to this law
in His life. One way in which He did this was by seeking
only the glory of God. In all He did and taught He humbly
gave His Father the glory. Even in death He glorified the
Father by making it possible for Him to forgive unworthy
sinners without compromising His holiness. Are the
activites of your life planned with a view to bringing God
glory?

5 JULY

*"But that the world may know that I love the
Father, and as the Father gave Me commandment,
even so I do" (John 14:31).*

Another way in which Jesus showed His love to the
Father was by keeping His Word. This involved more than
just obeying His commandments. You can obey without
a love for the commandments. Jesus loved the commandments. They were precious to Him. Therefore, He
guarded and defended them.

To the Psalmist, God's commandments were "more

desirable than gold. They are sweeter than honey dripping from a honeycomb" (*Psalm 19:10, The Living Bible*). This is not at all like the sophisticated deceiver who declares his love for God while rejecting selective sections of the inspired Word of God which don't fit into his philosophy of life.

Jesus went further than mere obedience to commandments. He made it His life's pursuit to discover those things that pleased the Father. He took the initiative to do those things that would please the Father and fulfill His will.

6 JULY

"The Son of God, who loved me, and delivered Himself up for me" (Galatians 2:20).

It was love that prompted the Father to send His Son, Jesus Christ, into our world to become our Savior and Lord (*John 3:16*). It was love that prompted the Son to obey the Father even unto death on the cross. It was love, not just responding to the Father's command, but also responding to our need as sinners. "Even if we were good, we really wouldn't expect anyone to die for us, though, of course, that might be barely possible. But God showed His great love for us by sending Christ to die for us while we were still sinners" (*Romans 5:7, 8, The Living Bible*).

This obviously is the divine love which does not act because the object of love is desirable or worthy. It acts because there is a need, and it is natural for divine love to respond to need. Divine love is a manifest concern for the well-being of the one loved. No price is too great to accomplish that objective. On the cross Jesus supremely manifested His love for us.

7 JULY

"The love of the Spirit" (Romans 15:30).

As love is the natural expression of the personality of God the Father and God the Son, so it is also of God the Holy Spirit. Love is manifested in all His actions. Never does He do or think anything which is out of harmony with Love.

It is the Holy Spirit who in a unique way is the one of the Trinity who communicates the love of God to us personally who believe. He sheds it abroad in our hearts and maintains an ever-present supply of love as He dwells within us *(Romans 5:5)*. This is how we know experientially that the Father and the Son love us. It is also the way in which we can express our love to God. "We love him, because he first loved us" *(1 John 4:19, KJV)*.

8 JULY

"But the fruit of the Spirit is love, joy, peace, patience, kindness, goodness, faithfulness, gentleness, self-control; against such things there is no law" *(Galatians 5:22, 23)*.

Prior to introducing the Spirit-filled life of fruitfulness, Paul discusses the repulsive life resulting from the works of the flesh *(Galatians 5:19-21)*. The flesh, even at its best, cannot produce a life that is pleasing to God. We must be freed from the frustration and failure of self-effort. But when freed, we must be sure to enter the sphere of life in the Spirit *(Galatians 5:16)*.

When the Spirit is in control, what we are and do will not be the result of effort. It will be the product of the

Spirit's presence and activity. We will love because He, as God, is love. It is the joy of the Spirit we will experience. His overwhelming peace will pervade our hearts. The word "fruit" is singular, showing us that the elements of character spoken of are all equally produced by the same Spirit. It is possible by effort to develop some of these elements of character. At least to man's satisfaction. But for all to be seen in a Christian, the Holy Spirit must be in control. He alone can produce a balanced and mature Christian life.

9 JULY

BUSINESS—PROVERBS (ten days to read)
"Buy truth, and do not sell it, get wisdom and instruction and understanding" (Proverbs 23:23).

In seeking to make his business one that would be known for character, dependability, and service-mindedness of the personnel, Herbert J. Taylor developed what is now known around the world as the *Four-way Test:* 1) Is it the truth? 2) Is it fair to all concerned? 3) Will it build goodwill and better friendships? 4) Will it benefit all concerned?

As you read Proverbs, note how these points are amplified and applied to daily life. You will probably find other practical guidelines as well. Billy Graham makes it a practice to read five Psalms and one chapter of Proverbs every day. He testifies that Proverbs has helped him more than anything else to understand how to relate to others.

God explains that what you get out of life is dependent upon what you put into it. Order your life according to God's guidelines and your life will be pleasing to God, meaningful to you, and profitable to others.

10 JULY

"Let us make man in our image" (Genesis 1:26).

Love, to be meaningful, must have an object. To be fulfilling it must have an object which responds in kind. Some feel this is why God made man, a creature who could understand and appreciate God's love and then by an act of His will respond. Without such a responsive creature upon which to lavish His love, God would have been unfulfilled, at least in this one dimension of His being.

You need not come to that conclusion if you understand the biblical doctrine of the Trinity. The one true God is three persons, each distinct from the other. These three divine persons have enjoyed a most intimate and unique relationship throughout eternities past. They have given and received and reciprocated their love for one another in an unsullied way. Never has their love for each other been blurred or broken. Never has it diminished or deteriorated. In their unity they have enjoyed the greatest dimension of fulfillment imaginable. They lacked nothing, and needed no one else to make their experience of love richer. No one could make it richer. They were completely self-sufficient in love.

11 JULY

"You shall love the Lord your God with all your heart, and with all your soul, and with all your mind. This is the great and foremost commandment" (Matthew 22:37, 38).

This commandment would be meaningless if it was not in the realm of possibility for man to obey it. Nowhere will you find such a command given to any other created thing or being. Only man was created with the mental, moral, and emotional faculties with which he could respond meaningfully to this command.

When God made humans in His image, He made them with the capacity to receive and experience His love. Man can appreciate God's overtures of love. And more, there is put within humans a desire to respond to God's love.

Since the fall of Adam into sin, men and women have been unable within themselves to express love to God *genuinely*. However, the capacity to do so can be acquired. Man must surrender himself to God and by faith trust in Christ to give him a new heart. This new heart, when enabled by the Holy Spirit's work, will be able to love God rightly.

12 JULY

"And this is love, that we walk according to His commandments" (2 John 6).

Jesus told His disciples, "If you love Me, you will keep My commandments" (*John 14:15*). Obedience and love go hand in hand as we walk with God. You cannot love God and at the same time disobey Him. If you love Him, you will be concerned about carefully fulfilling all of his directives. You will go even further by seeking to do things He hasn't stipulated, but which you know will please Him. You will want to serve God if you love Him.

Paul writes to the Thessalonians about their "labor of love." The word "labor" denotes intense or exhausting labor or toil. When you love God, you will labor diligently for Him. A lazy, easygoing lifestyle indicates an absence of love for God.

13 JULY

"We love Him because He first loved us"
(1 John 4:19, KJV).

We have already seen that God took the initiative in loving us by providing salvation for us while we were still sinners *(Romans 5:8; John 3:16)*. That initiative is looking for a response from us.

When we say we love Him, we are essentially expressing faith in Him. Peter puts it this way: "You love Him even though you have never seen Him; though not seeing Him, you trust Him; and even now you are happy with the inexpressible joy that comes from heaven itself. And your further reward for trusting Him will be the salvation of your souls" *(1 Peter 1:8, 9, The Living Bible)*.

To love Jesus Christ is to believe in Him. To believe in Him is to love Him. Love, like faith, to be meaningful and effectual must be active and responsive. Love which is not active is dead, just as faith without works is dead. The question all of us must ask ourselves is, "Do I love Jesus Christ actively?"

14 JULY

"Hate evil, you who love the Lord"
(Psalm 97:10).

Love is sensitive to the likes and dislikes of the one loved. Love studies the one loved to discover what will delight him or her and what will hurt him or her. To love God involves knowing His likes and dislikes, what will delight Him and what will hurt Him. You cannot love God and treat sin with indifference. He hates it. All sin. No sin is small to Him.

This hatred of sin includes the arena in which sin shows itself most freely. John says, "Stop loving this evil world and all that it offers you, for when you love these things you show that you do not really love God" (*1 John 2:15, The Living Bible*).

This is why Paul calls Christians to set their affection on things above, not the things of the world (*Colossians 3:2*). Demas neglected that warning and became a reject (*2 Timothy 4:10*). The world will draw you away from God and His concerns. That is why you cannot love both God and the world. (Compare *Matthew 6:24*.)

15 JULY

"If anyone says 'I love God,' but keeps on hating his brother, he is a liar; for if he doesn't love his brother who is right there in front of him, how can he love God whom he has never seen? And God himself has said that one must love not only God, but his brother too" (*1 John 4:20, 21, The Living Bible*).

In a stern way these verses strip away the sham and shallowness of a professed love for God which does not express itself in tangible actions of love to our brother. In fact the distinguishing mark of the Christian is clearly identified by Christ when He said, "A new commandment I give to you, that you love one another, even as I have loved you, that you also love one another. By this all men will know that you are My disciples, if you have love for one another" (*John 13:34, 35*).

God is never pleased with fine verbal expressions of love and devotion. He looks for a heart that responds as His does to the needs of those around us. "We know what real love is from Christ's example in dying for us. And so we also ought to lay down our lives for our Christian brothers. But if someone who is supposed to be a Christian has money enough to live well, and sees a brother in need, and won't help him—how can God's love be within *him*? Little children, let us stop just *saying* we love people; let us *really* love them, and *show it* by our *actions*" (*1 John 3:16-18, The Living Bible*).

16 JULY

"For God so loved the world, that He gave His only begotten Son, that whoever believes in Him should not perish, but have eternal life" (John 3:16).

This is known as the most profound statement in the Bible concerning the salvation God has provided for man. It presents love as the driving force which initiated God's action of providing salvation. It declared God's love to be unconditional. He loved the world; that is, He loved all who did, do, and ever will inhabit the world. He loved the great and small, the prominent and the insignificant, the rich and the poor, the strong and the weak, the healthy and the sick, the old and the young. No one can ever say, "God doesn't love me."

The extent of His love is shown by the sacrifice He was willing to make: "He gave His only begotten Son." The most precious possession He had He was willing to give in order to win us to Himself. That's why Paul prayed, "May your roots go down deep into the soil of God's marvelous love; and may you be able to feel and understand, as all God's children should, how long, how wide, how deep, and how high his love really is; and to experience this love for yourselves, though it is so great that you will never see the end of it or fully know or understand it. And so at last you will be filled up with God Himself" (*Ephesians 3:17-19, The Living Bible*).

17 JULY

"The love of Christ continuously constrains me" (2 Corinthians 5:14).

There is no greater motivating force than the love of

Christ. If we can begin to grasp what Jesus Christ has done for us, and that He did it because He loved us, we will be constrained to follow His example. His love is dynamic.

It will enable us to endure hardships and heartaches since He went all the way to the cross for us. It will encourage us to be patient and persistent since He often displayed those characteristics. It will enable us to be bold and confident in our work because we know He gloriously triumphed in our behalf.

Paul speaks of a motivation of fear (*2 Corinthians 5:11*). There is nothing wrong with doing things because of fear of the consequences if they are not done. But the love basis for motivation is far more positive and powerful.

18 JULY

"But I have this against you, that you have left your first love" (Revelation 2:4).

About a generation before John penned these penetrating words, Paul had prayed for this church—"Spiritual blessing be with all who have an undying love for our Lord Jesus Christ" (*Ephesians 6:24, Williams*). Paul was aware that the enemy of our souls is out to discredit and destroy our love relationship with Jesus Christ (*2 Corinthians 11:2, 3*).

Too often we are satisfied in our churches with mere orthodoxy, order, activity, or statistical accomplishments. These might all be praiseworthy, but if they are not infused with love and devotion to Jesus Christ they are nothing.

Note that they *left* their first love. Love is not lost. If it is not there, it has been left. "To love is in the power of the will" (Newell). That is why they were challenged to repent and return to their first love, or else their very testimony would be removed (*Revelation 2:5*).

19 JULY

BARRENNESS—ECCLESIASTES
(four days to read)

"Here is my final conclusion: fear God and obey his commandments, for this is the entire duty of man. For God will judge us for everything we do, including every hidden thing, good or bad" (Ecclesiastes 12:13, 14, The Living Bible).

"A magnificent desolation," is how astronaut James Aldrin described the moon soon after becoming the second man to step onto its surface.

Life on the merely human plane might also be described as a magnificent desolation. Solomon said that life is unproductive, unprofitable, and empty. It is a vicious, meaningless whirlwind that flings us around at will. Why get serious if death inevitably strips us of all we gain by effort?

From the divine perspective, however, we can see God at work in our world. He brings meaning and usefulness into life. That's why we are counseled, "Remember now thy creator in the days of thy youth" (*Ecclesiastes 12:1, KJV*). Before the drudgery of daily duties disillusions us we must get the right perspective on life.

Cultivate your consciousness of God's presence, remembering He knows your every thought, hears your every word, and sees your every deed. Then order your life accordingly. Otherwise you will know only barrenness in this life, and banishment in the life hereafter.

20 JULY

"Let us consider how to stimulate one another to love and good deeds" (Hebrews 10:24).
This word "consider" involves a diligent attentiveness

or continuous care. We should be looking out for each other's spiritual welfare. Our objective in keeping a close eye on each other is to provoke each other "to love and good deeds." The word translated *stimulate* or *provoke* has both a negative and a positive meaning. In certain contexts it could mean *irritate*. But here it is positive, meaning *to stir up* one another to do the right thing, the loving thing.

If we are to obey the above command we must be regular in our getting together as Christians (*Hebrews 10:25*). In fact, as the conditions in our world become more godless and demanding, we should meet more often. We need constant encouragement to live a life of love and good works.

21 JULY

*"And beyond all these things put on love,
which is the perfect bond of unity"*
(*Colossians 3:14*).

Love is the most important ingredient in a church that wants to know the blessing of God upon it. The inevitable differences of opinion when you get a group of people together to discuss purpose, goals, strategy, or finances, makes love indispensable.

Love will unite those who hold differing viewpoints. It is the "perfect bond of unity." You can exercise all the other virtues listed in Colossians 3:12, 13—compassion, kindness, humility, gentleness, patience, and forgiveness—and still not succeed. You need love to succeed. Love not only binds together and makes effectual the other virtues, but uses all the other virtues to bind together people of differing backgrounds, opinions and desires. *The Living Bible* translates this verse: "Most of all, let love guide your life, for then the whole church will stay together in perfect harmony" (*Colossians 3:14*).

22 JULY

"Speaking the truth in love, we are to grow up in all aspects into Him, who is the head, even Christ" (*Ephesians 4:15*).

Some people pride themselves upon always speaking the truth no matter what the consequences. God's Word indicates there should be a loving caution when the truth will no doubt hurt. There is a right time to speak the truth. There is also a right temperament to be exhibited when speaking the truth. Often there is a right setting for speaking the truth. Our objective in speaking the truth should be to build unity between brothers. Care must be taken not to compromise, but care must also be taken not to create unnecessary conflict. Every effort should be made to let love prevail.

Dialogue is important within the church. Through dialogue we get to know each other, our strengths and weaknesses, our burdens and blessings, our disappointments and opportunities. Communication is the name of the game. Yet we must be careful in our communication. Words can hurt as well as help. That's why we are to speak the truth in love.

23 JULY

BELOVED—THE SONG OF SOLOMON
(two days to read)

"I am my beloved's and I am the one he desires" (*Song of Solomon 7:10, The Living Bible*).

Love is an experience which cannot be adequately defined. Solomon, however, gives a vivid description of the love he shared with his beloved. Symbolically we can see described in this book the love we should have for our beloved Savior, Jesus Christ.

True love burns intensely. No sacrifice is too great, no road too dangerous, no opposition too strong. Love searches until it finds and when it finds it holds fast.

True love is intimate. It delights in discovering all there is to know about the beloved and in being discovered by the beloved. This necessitates a mutual submission and possession between the partners.

True love is also invincible. It cannot be conquered or subdued. It becomes purer and more precious when proved.

Can you honestly say, "I am my beloved's and my beloved is mine" (*Song of Solomon 6:3, The Living Bible*)? If not, you are robbing both yourself and Him. Seek the Lord until you find Him. Then surrender your all to Him. He will not disappoint you.

24 JULY

"He who has the bride is the bridegroom"
(John 3:29).

John the Baptist was being asked about his position in the plan of God. "Who are you?" His answer was both humble and beautiful. "I am a friend of the bridegroom and I am happy for Him." It was obvious that what he was saying is that Jesus Christ is the bridegroom who was making initial proposals to His bride. His bride would be the composite of all those who would respond positively to His proposals and identify with Him by faith as His followers.

Paul develops this theme further when he says, "'A man must leave his father and mother when he marries, so that he can be perfectly joined to his wife, and the two shall be one.' I know this is hard to understand, but it is an illustration of the way we are parts of the body of Christ" (*Ephesians 5:31, 32, The Living Bible*).

25 JULY

THE JUST JUDGE—ISAIAH
(nineteen days to read)

"For the Lord is our judge, The Lord is our lawgiver, The Lord is our king; He will save us" (Isaiah 33:22).

William Penn once said, "Right is right even if everyone is against it; and wrong is wrong, even if everyone is for it." Isaiah illustrates this as he speaks of the justice of God in His dealings with man. He points out that "the Lord is our judge . . . our lawgiver . . . our king; he will save us." As our king He has the right to judge us. As our lawgiver He knows how to rightly judge us. As our judge He deals righteously.

The reprobate are judged because they know not God and are not interested in knowing. The rebellious are judged because they know about God and His purpose but reject them both. The religious professors are judged because they come to God with religious rites but with hearts that are far from Him.

God's judgment, however, is overshadowed by His grace and tempered by His love. For as He punishes, He purifies. And as He purifies, He works out His divine plan.

26 JULY

"In the future there is laid up for me the crown of righteousness, which the Lord, the righteous Judge, will award to me on that day; and not only to me, but also to all who have loved His appearing" (2 Timothy 4:8).

Love for Christ prompts us to live in the glorious anticipation of His return. We should love His appearing.

There are many who are afraid of His appearing. They don't want Him to come while they are what they have allowed themselves to become. They are ashamed. They have not made adequate preparations. Their wedding garments are not ready.

John instructs us: "And as we live with Christ, our love grows more perfect and complete; so we will not be ashamed and embarrassed at the day of judgment, but can face him with confidence and joy, because he loves us and we love him too. We need have no fear of someone who loves us perfectly; his perfect love for us eliminates all dread of what he might do to us. If we are afraid, it is for fear of what he might do to us, and shows that we are not fully convinced that he really loves us" (*1 John 4:17, 18, The Living Bible*). Those who truly love Christ's appearing will receive the crown of righteousness.

27 JULY

"Let us rejoice and be glad and give the glory to Him, for the marriage of the Lamb has come and His bride has made herself ready" (Revelation 19:7).

When Jesus met with His disciples for the Last Supper, He said He would not drink with them of the fruit of the vine until a future day in His Father's kingdom (*Matthew 26:29*). The marriage supper of the Lamb will be the fulfillment of that promise. There the love relationship between Jesus Christ and His bride, made up of all those who have trusted in Him for salvation, will be complete.

John reveals that "it was given to her to clothe herself in fine linen, bright and clean; for the fine linen is the righteous acts of the saints" (*Revelation 19:8*). We are to prepare ourselves now in anticipation of that great festive day when we as the bride appear at the marriage supper of the Lamb. There love will be fulfilled.

28 JULY

*"Husbands, love your wives, just as Christ also
loved the church and gave Himself up for her"*
(*Ephesians 5:25*).

The man is the backbone of the family unit. He is the
final authority, under God, for decisions regarding the
family. As he makes decisions, however, he should carefully
consider how they might affect the various members of the
family. This consideration must be infused with love if the
welfare of each member is to be realized.

The place to begin is for a husband to love his wife. His
ideal is Jesus Christ, who loved the Church so much He
gave Himself for her. To correct a common error, the
husband is not to love his wife because she deserves it; he is
to love her whether she deserves it or not. Christ loved the
Church and gave Himself for her not because she was
worthy of such love and sacrifice. He loved her in spite of
her sin and imperfection. He died for her while she was yet
in her sin (*Romans 5:8*). That is how a husband is to love
his wife.

29 JULY

*". . . that they may encourage the young
women to love their husbands, to love their
children"* (*Titus 2:4*).

In other portions of the Bible dealing with family
relationships, the emphasis is on the importance of
husbands loving their wives and wives being subject to their
husbands. Here the emphasis is on the wife loving her
husband. This is easier if the husband loves the wife. But
she is to love him even if he doesn't show love to her. Love
takes the initiative.

Love is the strongest binding force in family relationships

and therefore should be cultivated by each member of the family.

Wives are also to love their children. This love will manifest itself in the provisions made, the sacrifices endured, and the discipline enforced for their well-being.

30 JULY

"We were exhorting and encouraging and imploring each one of you as a father would his own children" (1 Thessalonians 2:11).

The husband, who usually is also a father, has the further responsibility to love his children. This is not stated as such in the Bible, but it is implied in the instructions given to fathers by Paul: "Fathers, do not provoke your children to anger; but bring them up in the discipline and instruction of the Lord" (*Ephesians 6:4*). "Fathers do not exasperate your children, that they may not lose heart" (*Colossians 3:21*).

These two directives could be summarized: "Don't treat your children in an unloving manner, but work with them in love." Love seeks the benefit and enrichment of the one loved. Discipline is best exercised by one who loves, and should be exercised only as prompted by love. "If you refuse to discipline your son, it proves you don't love him; for if you love him you will be prompt to punish him" (*Proverbs 13:24, The Living Bible*). Instruction is merely talk unless motivated by and infused with love. Children will respond to loving instruction. They will resist nagging. Fathers, love your children.

31 JULY

"Children, obey your parents in the Lord, for this is right. Honor your father and mother" (*Ephesians 6:1, 2*).

To complete the triangle of love within the family, let us consider the importance of children loving their parents. Again there is no explicit statement concerning this, but it is strongly implied.

In Colossians 3:20 children are told to obey their parents in all things. Obedience and honor are characteristics of love. Jesus said, "If you love Me, you will keep My commandments" (*John 14:15*). If you love your parents, you will obey them. Regarding honor, Paul does not say to honor your parents only if they are honorable. No matter what your parents are like, you should live in such a way that others will honor your parents because of what they see in your life. This will communicate love to your parents in an unmistakable way.

1 AUGUST

"O Lord God of Israel, Thou art righteous"
(Ezra 9:15).

In many references God is presented as being righteous. Being righteous in His very nature, He always does what is right. It is inconceivable for God to be or do wrong. "But the Lord is there within the city, and he does no wrong. Day by day his justice is more evident, but no one heeds—the wicked know no shame" *(Zephaniah 3:5, The Living Bible).*

God created heaven and earth and instituted a moral government by which they would be ruled. To live in harmony with that moral government is to live in harmony with God. To rebel against His moral government results in certain consequences, including alienation from God.

The experience of Lucifer, later called Satan, vividly illustrates this point in regards to heaven *(Ezekiel 28:12-19; Isaiah 14:12-14).* The experience of Adam illustrates it in regard to the earth *(Genesis 3).* As unchanging as is God's righteous nature, so is His moral government. It is absolute.

2 AUGUST

"So then, the Law is holy, and the commandment is holy and righteous and good"
(Romans 7:12).

God reveals His righteousness and maintains His moral government through the just laws He has imposed upon those He created. The Law is a mirror, reflecting the righteousness of God. It is a measure by which we can determine what God requires for fellowship or harmony with Him.

It also reflects what is in line with His way of doing things. Why does He tell us not to steal? Because He is honest. Why does He demand that we not kill? Because man was created in His image. Why should we honor our father and mother? Because God gave them to watch over, guide, and provide for us. Why does God command us not to bear false witness? Because God always tells the truth. Yes, the commandments are like God. And they tell us how God expects us to live if we are to have fellowship with Him.

3 AUGUST

"He puts the righteous and the wicked to the test; he hates those loving violence. He will rain down fire and brimstone on the wicked and scorch them with his burning wind. For God is good, and he loves goodness; the godly shall see his face" (Psalm 11:5-7, The Living Bible).

Not only did God institute a moral government and impose just laws, He attached sanctions to these laws. A sanction, according to Webster, is "something that gives binding force to a law, as the penalty for breaking it, or a reward for carrying it out; provision of law that secures obedience."

God secures obedience to His laws in two ways. In many places throughout His Word He promises rewards to those who obey His commands (*Deuteronomy 7:9, 12, 13; 2 Chronicles 6:14; Psalm 58:11; Matthew 25:21; Romans 2:7; Hebrews 11:26*). This is called remunerative justice. You will also find ample references throughout His Word where He warns of inflicting punishment on those who disobey His commands (*Genesis 2:17; Exodus 34:7; Ezekiel 18:4; Romans 1:32, 2:8, 9; 2 Thessalonians 1:8*). This is called punitive justice. Both negatively and positively God establishes the fact that He will deal justly. It pays to obey.

4 AUGUST

"The Lord is righteous in all His ways, and kind in all His deeds" (Psalm 145:17).

Shedd throws further light on the difference between remunerative and punitive or retributive justice. He says: "Divine justice is originally and necessarily obliged to requite disobedience, but not to reward obedience . . . God cannot lay down a law, affix a penalty, threaten infliction, and proceed no further, in case of disobedience. The divine veracity forbids this . . . Hence, in every instance of transgression, the penalty of law must be inflicted, either personally or vicariously; either upon the transgressor or upon his substitute . . . Justice may allow of the substitution of one person for another, provided that in the substitution no injustice is done to the rights of any of the parties interested."[22]

This is the heart of the Good News. Jesus Christ was willing to take the penalty of the Law which we as sinners deserve. He allowed it to be inflicted upon Himself in our behalf. He took our place. Praise His holy name.

22. *Op. cit., Thiessen, p. 130.*

5 AUGUST

"Shall not the Judge of all the earth deal justly?" (Genesis 18:25).

The answer to Abraham's question is obvious. A God of righteousness can be counted on to do what is in harmony with the moral government He has established. Every law He imposed will stand. Every sanction to these will be carried out. God, as Judge, will not overlook anything.

It should be noted, however, that "justice, as an attribute of God, is devoid of all passion or caprice; it is vindicative, not vindictive. And so the righteousness and justice of the

God of Israel were made to stand out prominently as contrasted with the caprice of the heathen gods."[23] There is no privileged class of society whose misdeeds God overlooks, while He deals with others. We are all dealt with equitably by God, for "God is not one to show partiality" (*Acts 10:34*).

23. William Evans, *The Great Doctrines of the Bible* (Chicago: Moody Press, Moody Bible Institute of Chicago, © 1939), p. 41. Used by permission.

6 AUGUST

"Certainly this was a righteous man" (Luke 23:47, KJV).

Anyone who will reflect honestly upon the life of Jesus Christ as recorded in the Gospel narratives will come to the conclusion, "this was a righteous man." He always did what was right. Whether He encountered a group of children, a leper, a blind beggar, a religious leader, a tax collector, or a desperately sick woman pushing her way through a thronging crowd to touch Him, Jesus Christ always did the right thing. Though His mission was in a special sense to His own race, He ministered also to a scandalized Samaritan woman, to a Syrophoenician, and to other Gentiles. The one He described as the good Samaritan (in one of His parables) is a picture of Himself (*Luke 10:30-37*).

His heavenly Father said to His Son, "Thy Throne, O God, is forever and ever, and the righteous scepter is the scepter of His kingdom. Thou hast loved righteousness and hated lawlessness; therefore God, Thy God, hath anointed Thee with the oil of gladness above Thy companions" (*Hebrews 1:8, 9*).

7 AUGUST

*"He [the Father] gave Him [Jesus Christ]
authority to execute judgment, because He is
the Son of Man"* (John 5:27).

Two things mentioned here qualify Jesus Christ to
execute judgment. First, as the Son of Man He has
identified Himself with man's predicament. He was touched
with the feelings of our infirmities and tempted in all things
as we are. He can therefore empathize with us. This
qualifies Him to be objective. Second, He is identified with
the Father as divine. He has the authority to execute what
He in infinite wisdom determines is a proper judgment.
"For not even the Father judges any one, but He has given
all judgment to the Son" (John 5:22).

The one who is often depicted as meek and mild will one
day be firm and thorough in His responsibility to judge
everyone justly. In fact, He already is acting as Judge in the
life of the Church, walking in her midst, observing,
evaluating, and pronouncing His verdict (Revelation 2, 3).

8 AUGUST

*"Now judgment is upon this world; now the
ruler of this world shall be cast out"*
(John 12:31).

On the cross Jesus Christ was both the Judge and the one
judged. He judged Satan and destroyed his power over the
believer. He also judged the sins of the believer, putting
them and their eternal consequences away. The crucifixion
of Jesus Christ was the most unrighteous deed ever
committed by man. It was at the same time a righteous act
of God whereby He was able to deal with man's
predicament successfully without compromising His own
holiness.

The Holy Spirit takes this truth and uses it to "convict the world concerning sin, and righteousness, and judgment; concerning sin, because they do not believe in Me; and concerning righteousness, because I go to the Father, and you no longer behold Me; and concerning judgment, because the ruler of this world has been judged" (*John 16:8-11*). We should always live with the full consciousness that our great enemy, Satan, has already been judged. We are on the victorious Judge's side.

9 AUGUST

*"Now after a long time the master of those
slaves came and settled accounts with them"*
(Matthew 25:19).

This chapter begins with a challenge about preparedness. If you are not ready when the Master calls, it will be forever too late. Another consideration in the matter of preparedness is faithfulness in service. We are saved to serve. One day there will be an accounting. Jesus Christ, the righteous Judge, will reveal to us His estimate of our service. It will have to do with motives, methods, and effort. It will also reveal whether we served by faith or by mere self-effort.

Another factor that will come up for evaluation is effectiveness. If you received from God gifts and talents adequate to reach a certain number of people for Christ, then that number will be the standard by which actual results are measured. Christ declared that much will be required of him to whom much has been given (*Acts 20:35*). He also indicated His pleasure when one with little to offer gives what he can (*Luke 21:1-4*).

10 AUGUST

"But when I, the Messiah, shall come in my glory, and all the angels with me, then I shall sit upon my throne of glory. And all the nations shall be gathered before me. And I will separate the people as a shepherd separates the sheep from the goats, and place the sheep at my right hand, and the goats at my left" (Matthew 25:31-33, The Living Bible).

This is the third event mentioned in this chapter. First, the marriage supper (vv. 1-13); second, the judgment of servants (vv. 14-30); and third, the judgment of the living nations (vv. 31-46).

This is a specific judgment, not just a general judgment of good and bad. It is a judgment based on the way the nations have treated "these brothers of Mine" (v. 40). I believe Christ is speaking here of the way the Jewish remnant will be treated during the great tribulation yet to come. This judgment is rooted in a promise made centuries ago to Abraham (*Genesis 12:1-3*). The nations in existence at the close of this terrible period of judgment will be brought before the Great Judge, who will determine whether or not they will get to enter the millennial reign.

The promise made to Abraham is also relevant to us today. Those who show concern for the chosen people of God will see God showing concern for them. Those cursing the chosen people of God will experience the curse of God upon them. It is wise to pray for the peace of Jerusalem.

11 AUGUST

"And I saw the dead, the great and the small, standing before the throne, and books were opened; and another book was opened, which is the book of life; and the dead were judged from the things which were written in the books, according to their deeds" (Revelation 20:12).

This is the awesome picture of the great white throne judgment at which time Jesus Christ the Judge will pronounce the final, eternal doom upon all the unrighteous. Your position in life, great or small, will not be the issue in this judgment. This is also not a judgment at which you will find out whether or not you are saved. The saved will not face this judgment. Yet, the book of life will be opened; in it are all the names of those who are saved. Those who will stand before Jesus Christ at this great white throne judgment are those who do *not* have their names written in the book of life. They are the unrighteous. Their eternal doom is the second death, the lake of fire (*Revelation 20:11-15*).

This judgment is of "the dead" at the close of the millennium, in contrast to the judgment of the nations which is of "the living" and takes place at the beginning of the millennium.

12 AUGUST

"The dead were judged from the things which were written in the books, according to their deeds" (Revelation 20:12).

There are many who question whether there will be eternal, conscious punishment of the unrighteous. The Bible, however, makes it explicitly clear that such punishment is in store for the unrighteous.

Many who do believe this biblical truth are surprised to hear that there are degrees of punishment in the lake of fire. If your name is not in the book of life, then the record of your deeds will be read from the other books. A verdict will be based upon that record and an appropriate degree of punishment will be pronounced upon you.

When people were unrepentant in the cities where most of His miracles were done, Jesus Christ said, "Woe to you, Chorazin, and woe to you, Bethsaida! For if the miracles I did in your streets had been done in wicked Tyre and Sidon

their people would have repented long ago in shame and
humility. Truly, Tyre and Sidon will be better off on the
Judgment Day than you" (*Matthew 11:21, 22, The Living
Bible*).

13 AUGUST

THE DISILLUSIONED DISOBEDIENT—
JEREMIAH (fifteen days to read)

*"For My people have committed two evils:
They have forsaken Me,
The fountain of living waters,
To hew for themselves cisterns,
Broken cisterns,
That can hold no water" (Jeremiah 2:13).*

Disobedience inevitably leads to disillusionment, despair,
doom, and destruction. The heart of man, however, which is
"deceitful above all things, and desperately wicked"
(*Jeremiah 17:9*), seems driven to disobedience.

Since one act of disobedience makes the next one easier,
the disobedient heart gradually becomes disillusioned to the
point where the wrong seems right and the right wrong.
The heart thus deceived is unmistakably on the road to
destruction.

Is there any hope of deliverance? God says that the chain
reaction of going from one act of disobedience to another
must be broken. Also, a definite attempt must be made never
to disobey again. First, however, a positive surrender of
ourselves to God must be made (*Jeremiah 4:3, 4*). God is the
potter. We are but clay. We must become pliable clay free
from impurities so that God can form us into what He
desires (*Jeremiah 18:1-6*).

14 AUGUST

"Why has Satan filled your heart to lie to the Holy Spirit? . . . You have not lied to men, but to God" (Acts 5:3, 4).

The Holy Spirit is God. As God He is omniscient. He is also righteous. It is an insult to God to do something halfheartedly while leaving the impression outwardly that it was done wholeheartedly. God will not stand for such hypocrisy. The Holy Spirit will expose it as being at enmity with His indwelling presence. This enmity can grow in intensity to a point where you will suffer bitter consequences: *"For this reason many among you are weak and sick, and a number sleep [are dead]" (1 Corinthians 11:30).* This is precisely what happened to Ananias and Sapphira, only their death was dramatically sudden and caused great fear among all.

It grieves the Holy Spirit when Christians sin or, worse still, harbor sin in their hearts. He cannot let it go undealt with. And His dealings can lead to severe consequences. Never take lightly the righteousness of the Triune God.

15 AUGUST

"And He, when He comes, will convict the world concerning sin, and righteousness, and judgment" (John 16:8).

The Holy Spirit was sent by the Father and the Son to indwell the Church personally. He has a mission to the believer of purifying him and empowering him to live in a way which glorifies God.

He also has a mission to the lost in the world which He fulfills through the life and witness of believers. Believers are the instruments He uses to work on the lives of unbelievers. He has no feet but our feet, no hands but our hands, no tongue but our tongues. Our bodies, as believers, are temples of the Holy Spirit. As we move among those who are under the power of darkness the Holy Spirit causes our light to shine, thus exposing the need of those in darkness and providing a guide pointing to the solution to their need.

We must always let the Holy Spirit have His way in our lives so He can do His work of convicting, convincing, and ultimately converting the lost (*Ephesians 5:8-18*).

16 AUGUST

"In that they show the work of the Law written in their hearts, their conscience bearing witness, and their thoughts alternately accusing or else defending themselves" (Romans 2:15).

Man's conscience is an inner reflection of or witness to the Ten Commandments. Whether or not a person has ever heard or seen the commandments of God, he still has an inner sense of wrong and right regarding his actions. When God said, "You must not murder" (*Exodus 20:13, The Living Bible*), He was not introducing a new law. Murder had always been wrong. If we are angry at someone and feel like killing him, our conscience will condemn that feeling.

When God said, "You must not steal" (*Exodus 20:15, The Living Bible*), He was affirming something that was always true. Anyone old enough to distinguish what is his and what is someone else's knows instinctively that stealing is wrong. That's why stealing most often takes place at night or in the dark. When you have to hide or sneak about doing something, you know it is wrong. God's Word confirms and affirms what your conscience already has indicated as right or wrong.

17 AUGUST

"There is none righteous, not even one"
(Romans 3:10).

In his letter to the Romans, Paul develops the thesis that man is unrighteous. He begins by pointing out how corrupt the pagans are (chapter 1). Then he shows how sinful the privileged religious people are (chapter 2). To conclude his argument he quotes from Psalm 14:1-3 and 53:1-4 to show the universal nature of the sinfulness of man—there is not even one righteous person (chapter 3).

The prophet Isaiah pointed out that all of our righteousnesses—our attempts at doing righteous things—are as filthy rags in contrast to God's righteousness (*Isaiah 64:6*). This is hard for man to accept, but if he is honest with himself and God he must admit he is unworthy to present himself before a holy God.

Man's acceptance before God is never a matter of merit or worth. It is always a matter of mercy. If man got what he deserved, there would be no hope of reconciliation with God. This does not mean that every person is as bad as he could be, but rather that he is as bad off as he could be. He is definitely lost, spiritually dead.

18 AUGUST

"And may be found in Him, not having a righteousness of my own derived from the Law, but that which is through faith in Christ, the righteousness which comes from God on the basis of faith"
(Philippians 3:9).

This chapter of Philippians indicates that Paul was a good man: "as to the righteousness which is in the Law, found blameless" (v. 6). A person evaluating Paul's life might have considered him a righteous man. But Paul didn't look upon himself as possessing a personal righteousness derived from the Law. He had come to see the folly of self-righteousness. He wanted to know personally, and have others see in his life, a righteousness produced by the Holy Spirit as a direct result of faith in the Savior, Jesus Christ. This discussion is not dealing with a justifying righteousness, which is a right legal standing of the believer in Christ before God. Others can't see justifying righteousness. Rather, this discussion deals with a personal righteousness that is seen in the behavior of the believer.

The faith mentioned in this verse is not saving faith. Rather, this faith is a faith kindled, nourished, and maintained by Christ in those who are His. This faith appropriates the grace of God for *enablement to live* as He would have us live.

19 AUGUST

"By His doing you are in Christ Jesus, who became to us . . . righteousness"
(*1 Corinthians 1:30*).

Though every man is unrighteous in himself, he has the potential of righteousness. This righteousness is not a result of his own efforts, however. It is directly related to the character and work of another, Jesus Christ.

As the righteous Son of God who knew no sin, Jesus Christ was made sin for us. That is, our sin was placed on Him and He carried it to the cross where He died for our sin. All of this was done so that we might become the righteousness of God in Him (*2 Corinthians 5:21*). We are accepted in the Beloved (*Ephesians 1:6, KJV*). This is positional righteousness.

When I put my faith in Jesus Christ, God the Father no longer looks at me in myself with all of my flaws. He looks at me in Christ—and what He sees is the perfection of Jesus

Christ. Christ is my robe of righteousness which obviates my unrighteousness. This is why Paul declared, "In Him you have been made complete" (*Colossians 2:10*).

20 AUGUST

"For what the Law could not do, weak as it was through the flesh, God did: sending His own Son in the likeness of sinful flesh and as an offering for sin, He condemned sin in the flesh, in order that the requirement of the Law might be fulfilled in us, who do not walk according to the flesh, but according to the Spirit" (*Romans 8:3, 4*).

People who try to live according to the law will inevitably fail. That's why God sent His son to do a new thing through His death. "As an offering for sin, He condemned sin in the flesh." Christ did this so that the righteousness of the law might be fulfilled in us. Paul here uses the word *righteousness* in a collective sense, referring to *all* righteous requirements of the law. (Note *Luke 1:6; Romans 2:26*.)

Regarding the phrase, "might be fulfilled in us," Alford writes, *"find its full accomplishment,* not merely, be performed *by* us, for the apostle has a much deeper meaning, namely, that the *aim of God in giving the law* might be *accomplished* in us, in our sanctification, which is the ultimate end of our redemption (*Colossians 1:22; Ephesians 2:10*). The passive is used, to show that the work is not ours, but that of God by His grace."[24] Only when we walk with a full dependence on the Holy Spirit will this happen in us. We must not give room to the flesh.

24. Kenneth Wuest, *Word Studies in the Greek New Testament, Book 8, Romans* (Grand Rapids: Eerdmans, © 1955), p. 129. Used by permission.

21 AUGUST

"By the works of the Law no flesh will be justified in His sight; for through the Law comes the knowledge of sin" (Romans 3:20).

Man in himself is not and cannot be justified before God. He is devious, defiled, and deficient. God is like a straight line. In contrast man is crooked. If you were to describe God as being exactly vertical, you would have to describe man as leaning to one side or the other. Whenever God's righteousness charts a specific course of right behavior, you can be sure man will stray from it *(Isaiah 53:6)*. That's why Paul declared, "All have sinned and fall short of the glory of God" *(Romans 3:23)*.

God, nevertheless, declares throughout His Word that He desires fellowship with man. This presents God with a dilemma which can be resolved only by the good news of Jesus Christ. The barrier of sin which separates all men from God was removed by Jesus Christ on the cross. Now, through Christ, God can make the unrighteous righteous. Now man can be made fit for fellowship with God. This is what it means to be justified: to be forgiven of all sin and put back into a state of favor, acceptance, and privilege with God forever.

22 AUGUST

"Knowing that a man is not justified by the works of the Law but through faith in Christ Jesus, even we have believed in Christ Jesus, that we may be justified by faith in Christ, and not by the works of the Law; since by the works of the Law shall no flesh be justified" (Galatians 2:16).

There is a difference between the way we justify ourselves and the way God justifies us. We justify ourselves by explaining the reasons for our actions so that we look as though what we have done is right. When God justifies us, He does not declare that we are right when in fact we are wrong. He does not allow alibis. Sin is repugnant to God. He wants it removed, not just argued away.

Christ is the one who takes upon Himself our sin and failure. When we trust in Him, there is no need for argument or alibi or any kind of rationalizing. His substitutionary sacrifice satisfies God's righteousness so that our sin can be forgiven.

When a believer stands before God, he is accepted as if he never did anything wrong. This does not mean that God doesn't know that he did the wrong. Nor does it suggest that the believer doesn't remember he did wrong. Jesus and the Holy Spirit know the wrong. But in forgiveness God declares the sinner justified in His sight and chooses in love never to bring up that matter for consideration again.

23 AUGUST

"Now all these things are from God, who reconciled us to Himself through Christ, and gave us the ministry of reconciliation" (2 Corinthians 5:18).

A concept similar to justification, but which amplifies it, is revealed in the word *reconciliation*. To be in fellowship with God means you are enjoying your reconciliation with God. Man broke fellowship with God by going his own way, which is sin. God had to turn from man's sin because of His holiness. Man and God were moving in opposite directions. In love God found a way to turn around and face man again. Through Christ He could not only look to man but also seek him. In this, God was reconciled to man.

Now man too must turn, to face a holy God. This he can do only through Christ. This requires humbling himself, which is contrary to his sinful nature.

God's servants are sent forth motivated by the Holy Spirit to beg sinners "on behalf of Christ, be reconciled to God"

(2 *Corinthians 5:20*). "There is one God, and one mediator also between God and men, the man Christ Jesus" (1 *Timothy 2:5*). When God and man look each other in the face through Christ, they are reconciled. It is as though they had always been together.

24 AUGUST

"Him who was delivered up because of our transgressions, and was raised because of our justification" (*Romans 4:25*).

Our justification before God is the result of faith in the finished work of Christ on the cross. It is entirely "apart from works of the law" (*Romans 3:28*). Jesus paid it all. The Father, who with His foreknowledge knows all who would be justified as a result of His Son's sacrifice, proceeded to raise His Son from among the dead. This act of God demonstrated His acceptance of His Son's sacrifice as being adequate to fully justify all who would believe.

The resurrection of Jesus Christ is our guarantee of being forgiven, cleansed, justified, and ultimately glorified. We would never know with certainty that we have eternal life if Jesus Christ had not risen from the dead. Praise God, He arose! Praise God we can know that we have eternal life (*1 John 5:13*).

25 AUGUST

"Therefore having been justified by faith, we have peace with God through our Lord Jesus Christ" (*Romans 5:1*).

The most wonderful thing about salvation is the

assurances of the peace we have in Christ. Having been justified, we have peace with God. In our natural state we are at enmity with God. We cannot please Him (*Romans 8:7, 8*). Jesus Christ as our mediator arbitrates a peaceful state between man and God. Jesus Christ is our peace (*Ephesians 2:14*). He put enmity to death on the cross (*Ephesians 2:16*).

As we become aware of this great work of our Savior, we begin to experience and enjoy the peace of God in our hearts. This then becomes the basis of our becoming peacemakers, the identifying characteristic of sons of God (*Matthew 5:9*).

Peace *with* God is a settled state for time and eternity, once one has trusted in Christ. The peace *of* God is bestowed and maintained as we "walk in the light as He Himself is in the light" (*1 John 1:7*).

We are to let this peace rule or referee in our hearts (*Colossians 3:15*). If we are not experiencing peace, we are allowing something which does not please God. It must be corrected if peace is to be restored.

26 AUGUST

"Jesus said to him, 'I am the way, and the truth, and the life; no one comes to the Father, but through Me' " (*John 14:6*).

It indeed is possible for sinful men to be reconciled to God. But it must be declared emphatically that there is only one way for this reconciliation to take place. God, being just, must operate on a just basis when He justifies men.

It is common for uninformed people to feel that there are many ways to reach God. But the writer of the Proverbs twice proclaimed, "There is a way which seems right to a man, but its end is the way of death" (*14:12; 16:25*). Peter also made it clear that "there is salvation in no one else; for there is no other name under heaven that has been given

among men, by which we must be saved" (*Acts 4:12*). And
Paul points out, "For there is one God, and one mediator
also between God and men, the man Christ Jesus"
(*1 Timothy 2:5*).

This might seem exclusive or unloving. What about the
millions who have never heard of Jesus Christ? The Bible
declares that God "desires all men to be saved and to come
to the knowledge of the truth" (*1 Timothy 2:4*). The good
news is that anyone and everyone who comes to God
through Christ will be saved.

27 AUGUST

*"Oh, dear children, don't let anyone deceive you
about this: if you are constantly doing what is
good, it is because you are good, even as he is. But if you
keep on sinning, it shows that you belong to Satan, who
since he first began to sin has kept steadily at it"* (*1 John 3:7,
8, The Living Bible*).

God is righteous in Himself and in all that He does. Man
is unrighteous but can be delivered from his unrighteous
state and tendency, and can be righteous in and through
Christ.

Satan, who fell from his lofty state as first created, is
unrighteous in all his ways and is incorrigible. He neither
can nor wants to be in harmony with God. He is opposed
to all that God is and has purposed. He relentlessly
endeavors to thwart God's foreordained plan. And as long as
God allows Satan freedom to function as the prince of the
power of the air and as the god of this world, you can be
sure he will do all he can to withstand the work of God in
our lives.

That's why Paul encourages us to put on the whole
armor of God so that we can maintain a righteous life in an
unrighteous world (*Ephesians 6:10-18*).

28 AUGUST

JUST LIGHT YOUR CANDLE—
LAMENTATIONS (one day to read)

"His compassion never ends. It is only the Lord's mercies that have kept us from complete destruction. Great is his faithfulness; his lovingkindness begins afresh each day" (*Lamentations 3:22, 23, The Living Bible*).

A young doctor leaving for service in a war torn country was asked a difficult question: "What can you do against war, famine, and flood?"

"When it is dark around me," he replied, "*I* do not curse the darkness, I just light my candle."

Jeremiah knew Israel deserved the punishment they got. But he couldn't stand idly by and watch the punishment of his people without deep pangs of passion. Though the scene was dark and dismal, he came to realize that God promised to be faithful (*Lamentations 3:22, 23*). He could be trusted, even when all seemed desolate, by those who turned to Him wholeheartedly. To hold up the light of that truth was enough.

A laborer for God, if he is to be faithful and fruitful, must identify himself with his people and their need, and bring the promises of God to bear upon both. He must be touched with the things that touch his people. And because of his trust in the faithfulness of God, he must labor on in love till he can labor no more.

29 AUGUST

THE PUNITIVE PURGE—EZEKIEL
(thirteen days to read)

"And I shall make you pass under the rod, and I shall bring you into the bond of the covenant" (*Ezekiel 20:37*).

God abhors whatever is defiled or impure. The children of Israel, who were to be a people holy unto the Lord, compromised their high standards and committed idolatry. In this they defiled themselves and became impure. Therefore, God had to fling them into the furnace of affliction. God's purpose, however, was not mere punishment. It involved restoration as well.

When God punishes His own, He always does it to purge them of that which defiles and disqualifies them for fellowship with Him. Don't resist God's punitive purge. Resistance only intensifies and prolongs it, as in the case of Israel (*Ezekiel 24:13*). Respond to chastening by renouncing your evil way and returning to the Lord with all your heart. Such a response will always lead to restoration.

30 AUGUST

"For rulers are not a cause of fear for good behavior, but for evil. Do you want to have no fear of authority? Do what is good, and you will have praise from the same; for it is a minister of God to you for good" (*Romans 13:3, 4*).

Knowing man's evil nature and the human tendency to take unfair advantage of one another, God established government to exercise law and order among people. Unchecked and undisciplined nations will destroy themselves. Under God, governments are to establish and administer laws which keep people from doing wrong to one another. When citizens live good lives, they will have praise from such governments. But if they live evil lives, they have reason to be afraid, "for it [the government] does not bear the sword for nothing; for it is a minister of God, an avenger who brings wrath upon the one who practices evil" (*Romans 13:4*).

Some might question submitting to governments which obviously do not fulfill the description of governments as Paul presents it. It should be noted that the government of Rome during Paul's lifetime left much to be desired as far as righteousness is concerned. Yet Paul encouraged the believers of his day to be subject to the government which God had established for them (*Romans 13:1, 2*).

31 AUGUST

"We must obey God rather than men"
(*Acts 5:29*).

Peter agreed with Paul that Christians, for the Lord's sake, are to "obey every law of your government: those of the king as head of the state, and those of the king's officers, for he has sent them to punish all who do wrong, and to honor those who do right" (*1 Peter 2:13, 14, The Living Bible*). Peter lived under the rule of the evil Roman government, as did Paul.

There are times, however, when they had to make a choice between what the rulers of their day insisted upon and what God had commanded. God told them to preach the good news to every living person. The authorities commanded Peter and his associates to keep quiet about the good news (*Acts 4:18; 5:28*). Should they submit to human authority or obey God?

Whenever there is a conflict between those two authorities in our lives, we must obey God rather than man. John Bunyan felt he had to obey God, and he decided to accept what human government would do to him for obeying God. Human authorities put him in prison for preaching. While in prison he wrote *Pilgrim's Progress*, which has been an all-time best seller. No authority can frustrate the purposes of God. Believe that and prove it by obeying God even when obedience is costly.

1 SEPTEMBER

"My glory I will not give to another"
(Isaiah 48:11).

There are many degrees of glory, but the glory attributed to God is unique. And God is jealous for that glory. He will not give it to or share it with another.

Many have at times compared the glory of their heathen gods with that of the true God, always only to discover the wrath of God manifest in retaliation (*1 Samuel 5:1-5*). And when those who didn't know the glory of God irreverently took the ark of God into their land, plagues and other catastrophes engulfed them (*1 Samuel 5:6-12*).

Yes, it is important to understand that the glory of the true God is unique and demands our humble recognition and reverence. This is precisely what the old Presbyterian catechism says: "What is the chief end of man? The chief end of man is to glorify God and to enjoy Him forever." You cannot enjoy Him unless you glorify Him.

2 SEPTEMBER

"While My glory is passing by . . . I will put you in the cleft of the rock and cover you with My hand until I have passed by" (*Exodus 33:22*).

Moses was on intimate, face to face terms with God. Yet down in his heart there was a desire to know God and His ways better. In dialogue Moses got bold and asked to see the glory of God (*Exodus 33:18*). God replied that He would do many gracious things for Moses but one thing He wouldn't do is show him His glory. Why? "You may not see the glory of my face, for man may not see me and live" (*Exodus 33:20, The Living Bible*).

Man has seen many reflections of God's glory: the burning bush, the glorious deliverance from Egypt (*Numbers 14:22*), the pillar of fire by night and the pillar of smoke by day as they traveled through the wilderness, etc. Even today we can say with the Psalmist, "The heavens are telling of the glory of God" (*Psalm 19:1*). But God in His pristine glory no man can see and live. We must remember that fact when we approach and address God. He graciously condescends to adapt His manifestations to our finite comprehension. But there is always more, infinitely more, of God and His glory than we in our lifetime will ever know.

3 SEPTEMBER

"The glory which I ever had with Thee before the world was" (John 17:5).

There was a glory which Jesus Christ shared with the Father throughout eternity past. This glory is inherent in deity. It is not something God manufactures or assumes. There never was a time when God did not exude this glory. This is what Paul refers to in Philippians 2:6 when he says that Jesus "existed in the form of God." The word "form" conveys the idea that what is inwardly or inherently real is outwardly manifest.

What might be outwardly displayed of the glory of God is the same as what is intrinsically and eternally present in the very being and nature of God. This is not a fading glory. It always has blazed with an infinite splendor, and it always will. That's why Jesus Christ had to come from heaven's dazzling glory to reveal the Father whom no man had seen or could see with mortal eyes and live.

4 SEPTEMBER

"The city has no need of the sun or of the moon to shine upon it, for the glory of God has illumined it" (*Revelation 21:23*).

When we think of heaven we may visualize material splendor, for we have read of the streets of gold, foundation stones of the holy city "inlaid with gems" (*Revelation 21:19, The Living Bible*), gates made of a single pearl, a river of the water of life which is clear as crystal, and the tree of life bearing fruit every month. But all of that combined would not make heaven glorious were God not present there. It is His own glory that makes heaven so wonderful. His glory is heaven's splendor. His glory is heaven's light. His glory is the focal point of the worship of heaven's inhabitants. The best way to prepare for heaven is to reflect upon the glory of our God.

5 SEPTEMBER

"Glorify Thou Me together with Thyself, Father, with the glory which I ever had with Thee before the world was" (*John 17:5*).

This is hard to understand when you compare it with John 1:14: "And the Word became flesh, and dwelt among us, and we beheld His glory, glory as of the only begotten from the Father, full of grace and truth." Here John reported the disciples' seeing a unique glory in the Son of Man which identified Him also as God. Yet Jesus Christ indicates that He laid aside the glory which was shared by Him with the Father, and was asking that it be returned as a culmination to His earthly sojourn.

Obviously the effulgence of glory which would render a

human beholder dead (*Exodus 33:20*) was not present during Jesus' earthly life. It was the outward manifestation of inner reality of being that Jesus did not grasp and hold on to. It was that manifestation that He could lay aside without becoming less than what He was (*Philippians 2:6-9*). However, when He had fulfilled His earthly mission and was returning to heaven, He had that rightful manifestation of glory restored. Worthy is the Lamb!

6 SEPTEMBER

"He was transfigured before them; and His face shone like the sun, and His garments became as white as light" (*Matthew 17:2*).

Peter never forgot this experience (*2 Peter 1:16-18*). I'm sure James and John never did either. They saw the glory of Jesus Christ in a way that was not normally evident. The word "transfigured" refers to outward manifestation of inward reality. A body had been prepared for Jesus Christ's earthly existence (*Hebrews 10:5*). His body of flesh was as it were a veil (*Hebrews 10:20*) which covered or clothed His glory. On the mount of transfiguration, that fleshly veil became transparent and His glory burst through.

Yet it evidently was not the complete effulgence of divine glory, since the reflexes of the disciples were not the same as when within moments "a bright cloud overshadowed them; and behold, a voice out of the cloud, saying, 'This is My beloved Son, with whom I am well pleased; hear Him!'" (*Matthew 17:5*). At that the disciples fell on their faces in fear. Not until back in heaven, having victoriously completed His mission, did He have the full manifestation of His glory restored. Praise Him for His great self-emptying act to become our Savior.

7 SEPTEMBER

"I turned to see . . . one like a son of man . . .
and when I saw Him, I fell at His feet as a dead
man" *(Revelation 1:12-17).*

John had seen Jesus' transfiguration during His earthly life. In the Revelation He sees Jesus Christ in His restored glory. Words are hardly capable of describing what John saw. But the overwhelming impact left him stunned, prostrate as a dead man at Christ's feet.

"John did not intend his description of Christ to be taken with a strict literalness, which here would be grotesque. The figures of speech are rather to be translated into the various characteristics and functions of Christ. His clothing represents royal priesthood, His white hair eternal age, His flaming eyes the piercing gaze of omniscience, His bronze-like feet the stamping down of judgmental activity, His thunderous voice divine authority, the two-edged sword His word, and His shining face the glory of His deity."[25]

8 SEPTEMBER

"If you are reviled for the name of Christ, you
are blessed, because the Spirit of glory and of
God rests upon you" *(1 Peter 4:14).*

Dr. Wuest translates the last of this verse as follows: "The Spirit of the Glory, even the Spirit of God is resting with refreshing power upon you." This is based upon the Greek construction on which Vincent elaborates in his word

25. Robert H. Gundry, *A Survey of the New Testament* (Grand Rapids: Zondervan, © 1970), p. 368. Used by permission.

26. Marvin R. Vincent, *Word Studies in the New Testament,* Vol. 1 (New York: Charles Scribner's Sons, © 1906), pp. 663, 664. Used by permission.

studies: "The repetition of the article identifies the spirit of God with the spirit of glory: the spirit of glory, and *therefore* the spirit of God: who is none other than the spirit of God himself."[26]

Thus the Word of God identifies the Holy Spirit with God the Father and God the Son as the one true *glorious* God. Throughout the eternities the Holy Spirit shared in the manifestation of the intrinsic glory of God. His very name suggests this, but Peter clearly declares it as a basis for our comfort in the face of persecution. The glory of the Holy Spirit, when contemplated, is a refreshing source of power for the Christian.

9 SEPTEMBER

"The ministry of death, in letters engraved on stones, came with glory" (2 Corinthians 3:7).

When Moses went up the holy mountain to meet with God, the *shekina* glory engulfed him. For forty days he remained in the glorious presence of God. When God had a second time given him the Ten Commandments engraved on stones, Moses came down from the mountain to deliver the commandments to the people. Not realizing the effect of being in God's presence for so long, he was surprised to find that his own face now had a glow to it.

This phenomenon brought fear to Aaron and all the sons of Israel. But Moses called them to himself and taught them all that God had shared with him. After his address he put a veil over his face, Paul says, to hide the fact that the glow diminished with time. Whenever he went into God's presence he would remove the veil. Then he would put it back on after delivering whatever message God gave him. The glory of the Law was a fading glory (*2 Corinthians 3:13*).

10 SEPTEMBER

"For if the ministry of condemnation has glory, much more does the ministry of righteousness abound in glory" (2 Corinthians 3:9).

As we have already seen, the glory that accompanied the law faded. Now Paul declares that the glory of the gospel not only does not fade, it surpasses the glory of the Law (*2 Corinthians 3:10, 11*). What makes the glory of the gospel so much superior? It is a glory which remains and can be built upon or added to. As a Christian reads or listens to God's Word, he sees the glory of God reflected in it (*2 Corinthians 3:18*). The Holy Spirit begins a work of internalizing the truth of God in a believer and then working it out in the believer's life. That's what it means to be "transformed into the same image."

Paul describes this process as being "from glory to glory." The glory of the gospel is what God's Spirit does of a transforming nature in the life of the believer. This is a progressive work in which glory is added to glory to make the glory more intensive. The Law could not do that.

11 SEPTEMBER

DARE TO BE DIFFERENT—DANIEL
(three days to read)

"But Daniel made up his mind that he would not defile himself with the king's choice food or with the wine which he drank; so he sought permission from the commander of the officials that he might not defile himself" (Daniel 1:8).

Phillips Brooks might have had Daniel in mind when he said, "Do not pray for easy lives. Pray to be stronger men. Do not pray for tasks equal to your powers. Pray for powers equal to your tasks."

Early in life Daniel purposed in his heart that he would not defile himself. He was joined by Shadrach, Meshach, and Abednego, who likewise were unwavering in their determination to stand for God.

The book of Daniel is full of prophetic utterances. God had to have a clear channel to make these revelations known. Such a channel He found in Daniel. He was tried, tempered, and trustworthy. His prayer life was consistent and his consecration complete. He was willing to pay any price to do God's will. And he was humble enough to give God the glory for all his accomplishments.

"Dare to be a Daniel!" Purpose in your heart to be a clear channel through which God's Word goes forth unhindered and unmarred by the obstructions of sin. Make yourself available to do God's bidding, no matter what the cost.

12 SEPTEMBER

"And when the Chief Shepherd appears, you will receive the unfading crown of glory"
(*1 Peter 5:4*).

Much is not clear about what this "crown of glory" refers to, but one thing is certain—it is promised by God to faithful servants. It is a reward which is to be distinguished from the experience all believers will have of being glorified. As is true of our glorified bodies, this crown possesses a glory which is unfading.

This crown will be received as the ultimate exaltation for those who have humbled themselves in life under the mighty hand of God (*1 Peter 5:6*). It will be worn, not in a proud, arrogant fashion, but in such a way that the Chief Shepherd will be honored by the wearer. There is every indication in Scripture that this crown will identify the realm of authority over which the wearer will rule (*Matthew 25:14-29*). This is not the only reason, nor even the primary reason, but it is one of the reasons why you should take care how you serve when called of God to lead a flock of believers.

13 SEPTEMBER

"Looking for the blessed hope and the appearing of the glory of our great God and Savior, Christ Jesus" (Titus 2:13).

There is coming a day when these mortal eyes will behold the glory of our great God and Savior, Christ Jesus. It will not be an extensive look, for in the moment we behold, something wonderful is going to take place. "But we know that when he appears, we shall be like him, for we shall see him as he is" (*1 John 3:2, NIV*).

Paul declares "we shall all be changed, in a moment, in the twinkling of an eye, at the last trumpet" (*1 Corinthians 15:51-52*). Yes, when He comes in His glory and we behold Him, He "will transform the body of our humble state into conformity with the body of His glory, by the exertion of the power that He has even to subject all things to Himself" (*Philippians 3:21*).

This is our blessed hope. This is our full salvation. This is that for which we were created. Oh, the joy that day will bring. "And everyone who has this hope fixed on Him purifies himself, just as He is pure" (*1 John 3:3*).

14 SEPTEMBER

THE LOVING LORD—HOSEA (three days to read)

"I will cure you of idolatry and faithlessness, and my love will know no bounds . . . . I will refresh Israel like the dew from heaven" (Hosea 14:4, 5, The Living Bible).

God is love. Nowhere is this more graphically portrayed than in Hosea where you will see love's agony, action, and accomplishment.

God cannot condone sin. He must condemn sin and the sinner. Condemning the object of His love, however, is agonizing.

God's strong love spurns Him to action directed toward making the sinner aware of his utter need for help. He sets up one blockade after another in the sinner's path until the sinner is utterly frustrated and friendless. Then God extends His loving invitation to receive and reconcile the sinner unto Himself. The accomplishment of God's love is seen when the sinner comes to Him in surrender.

Hosea teaches us that God loves with a love that will not let go. We should therefore turn from self and sin and let God be Lord of all, once for all, and all the time. Only then will we know Him as our ever-loving Lord.

15 SEPTEMBER

"Solomon in all his glory did not clothe himself like one of these" (Matthew 6:29).

Solomon was a man of wisdom and phenomenal wealth. He had everything going for him. Yet in all his glory he was less attractive than the lilies of the field. The same could be said for all of mankind. At best we are less than we could be. "All . . . fall short of the glory of God" (*Romans 3:23*).

Paul acknowledges the fact that "nothing good dwells in me, that is, in my flesh" (*Romans 7:18*). Yet when a person is called by God into relationship with Him, he is caught up in a process that culminates in glorification. Paul describes the process as follows: "For whom He foreknew, He also predestined to become conformed to the image of His Son, that He might be the first-born among many brethren; and whom He predestined, these He also called; and whom He called, these He also justified; and whom He justified, these He also glorified" (*Romans 8:29, 30*).

16 SEPTEMBER

"That He might present to Himself the church in all her glory, having no spot or wrinkle or any such thing; but that she should be holy and blameless" (*Ephesians 5:27*).

An interesting emphasis in the original clarifies what Paul is saying. "It is Christ Himself who is to present the Church, and it is to Himself He is to present it. He is at once the Agent and the End or Object of the presentation . . . The idea, as the context suggests, is that of the Bridegroom presenting or setting forth the bride. The presentation in view, which is given here as the final object of Christ's surrendering of Himself to death, and (by use of the aorist) as a single definite act, cannot be anything done in the world that now is, but must be referred to the future consummation, the event of the *Parousia* (the Rapture)."[27]

The second part of the verse focuses on the nature of the Church at the time of this presentation. She is glorious. That is, she is free from all moral spots or wrinkles or any such thing. On the positive side, she is holy and blameless. The Church is not that yet, but when Christ comes to rapture her, her final preparations will be made so that this promise will be fully accomplished.

17 SEPTEMBER

LET'S REALLY REPENT—JOEL
(one day to read)

"That is why the Lord says, 'Turn to me now, while there is time. Give me all your hearts. Come with fasting, weeping, mourning. Let your remorse tear at your hearts and not your garments.' Return to the Lord your God, for

27. *Op. cit.*, Wuest, *Ephesians and Colossians*, p. 132.

he is gracious and merciful. He is not easily angered; he is
full of kindness, and anxious not to punish you" (Joel
2:12, 13, The Living Bible).

When accused of rubbing the fur the wrong way because
of the way he preached, Billy Sunday would answer, "I do
not! Let the cat turn around." That is what repentance is all
about: turning around. It is a matter of the heart where the
real issues of life are determined (*Proverbs 4:23*).

But the heart is approached through the head. So Joel
gives the heart reasons for repenting. When God is
forgotten, the beautiful is made barren, the delightful is
destroyed, and the garden becomes a wilderness. These
outward manifestations of being abandoned by God are sure
signs that we need to repent. Joel then spells out the remedy
for this condition. Our hearts must be made available for
God to work on them, in them, and through them. He
changes the outside by changing the inside.

When the repentant heart is renewed, it will inspire the
hands. Once healed ourselves, we are instructed to help
others. Repentance is not the result of works, but it does
result in works.

18 SEPTEMBER

BEWARE: THE DEVIL'S WORKSHOP—
AMOS (two days to read)

"Woe to those who are at ease in Zion, and to those who
feel secure in the mountain of Samaria . . ." (Amos 6:1).

We all know that the devil tempts every man. Not as
many know that the idle man tempts the devil. Someone
has said, "An idle life is the devil's workshop." Amos, who
saw the evil consequences of this in Israel, cried out, "Woe
to them that are at ease in Zion" (*Amos 6:1*).

Israel's religious leaders and the rich had squeezed enough
out of the poor to live in luxury. Thus, they were careless,
calloused, and cruel in their brotherly relationships.

In their religious life they were diligent but not devoted,

formal but faithless, sensual but not spiritual. And God
hated this! Having put far away the thought of an evil day
of judgment, they lived for themselves.

Denouncing their way of life, Amos challenged them to
prepare to meet their God by seeking Him and His way
with all their hearts.

19 SEPTEMBER

*"The one whose coming is in accord with the
activity of Satan, with all power and signs and
false wonders"* (2 Thessalonians 2:9).

Satan tried once in the distant past to make himself like
God. He continues to cherish that dream. With that in
mind he will groom someone, yet in the future, referred to
in the Bible as "the man of rebellion . . . the son of hell. He
will defy every God there is, and tear down every other
object of adoration and worship. He will go in and sit as
God in the temple of God, claiming that he himself is God"
(2 Thessalonians 2:3, 4, The Living Bible).

Paul is no doubt referring to the antichrist of whom
Daniel prophesied in Daniel 7:25; 8:25; 11:36-39. John also
spoke of his rise to prominence under the direction and
dynamic of that old dragon, Satan. He would not only
blaspheme God, but be worshiped by man. And to make
sure that all join in this worship, another beast, the false
prophet, performing great signs and exercising great powers
of deception, institutes the mark of the beast as a means of
getting the necessities of life. Anyone living at that time
who wants to exist must have the mark of the beast put on
his forehead and demonstrate his allegiance to the beast by
worshiping him (*Revelation 13*). What a dreadful day that
will be.

20 SEPTEMBER

THE LAW OF THE SEED—OBADIAH
(one day to read)

"The Lord's vengeance will soon fall upon all Gentile nations. As you have done to Israel, so will it be done to you. Your acts will boomerang upon your heads" (Obadiah 15, The Living Bible).

"Be not deceived; God is not mocked: for whatsoever a man soweth, that shall he also reap" (*Galatians 6:7*). This truth is seen in Obadiah's prophecy against Edom. Edom was a proud people. Their valleys were filled with rich soil. Surrounding them were high, rugged mountains. From these secure dwelling places the Edomites went forth to plunder surrounding nations. Israel was often their target. When they had struck and stolen what they could get, they retreated to the safety of their cities.

Obadiah pointed to their pride and declared that their impressive strongholds would be destroyed by Almighty God. He predicted that what they were doing to others would one day happen to them. And history confirmed the prediction.

The law of the seed still operates today, so take care what you sow.

21 SEPTEMBER

THE POUTING PROPHET—JONAH
(one day to read)

"While I was fainting away, I remembered the Lord; and prayer came to Thee, into Thy holy temple" (Jonah 2:7).

Dwight L. Moody once confided, "I have more trouble with D. L. Moody than with any other man I ever met." Jonah would have to say the same about his own life. He thought everything should go exactly the way he wanted it to go. When it didn't, he pouted childishly.

Pouting is a far too common ailment among God's people. Its cause is self-reliance and self-interest. Its cure is found in putting God's interests first, the other person's second, and your own last. Then it won't be hard to do what God asks of you. You will also be able to praise God for the results no matter what they are.

When you feel like pouting, start praising.

22 SEPTEMBER

A DELIVERING DISCIPLINE—MICAH
two days to read)

"I will bear the indignation of the Lord because I have sinned against Him, until He pleads my case and executes justice for me. He will bring me out to the light, and I will see His righteousness" (Micah 7:9).

The cause of some illnesses can be removed only by the knife of the doctor. When he operates he does not cut to hurt, but to heal. Similarly, when God saw Israel's drastic spiritual condition He prescribed the painful surgical experience of the captivity.

Micah's task was to proclaim this impending judgment. But shining through the dismal forecast was the promise of restoration. In reading the book you will learn to let God choose the discipline suited for your deliverance. Don't try to be delivered from the discipline, for deliverance comes through the discipline. Endure it. Then thank Him for it.

23 SEPTEMBER

"And every one who has this hope fixed on Him purifies himself, just as He is pure" (1 John 3:3).

Holy living is based on the truth that since God is holy, his followers should be also. This is intensified when we realize that we are someday going to come face to face with this holy God.

It has not yet appeared what we are going to become. We are still earthly in many of our attitudes and actions. We are encouraged to "set [our] sights on the rich treasures and joys of heaven where [Christ] sits beside God in the place of honor and power. Let heaven fill your thoughts; don't spend your time worrying about things down here" (*Colossians 3:1, 2, The Living Bible*). In another book, Paul instructs us to "think on things which are pure" (*Philippians 4:8*). Even though we presently must discipline ourselves in this way, we know that when Jesus Christ appears "we shall be like Him, because we shall see Him just as He is" (*1 John 3:2*). We will have these bodies of our humble state transformed "into conformity with the body of His glory" (*Philippians 3:21*).

24 SEPTEMBER

GOD'S WOESOME WRATH—NAHUM
(one day to read)

"A jealous and avenging God is the Lord; the Lord is avenging and wrathful. The Lord takes vengeance on His adversaries, and He reserves wrath for His enemies" (*Nahum 1:2*).

If you have never read Jonathan Edwards' sermon, "Sinners in the Hands of an Angry God," then read Nahum. The same basic point is made in both, even though the particulars differ.

The people of Nineveh had experienced God's forgiveness and favor when they repented under Jonah's ministry. But their repentance was short-lived. Now their hearts were hardened. Therefore, God's wrath was poured out upon them and Nineveh was laid waste.

Two truths to note in Nahum's message are: first, God is

slow to anger; second, God is jealous. There is a point
beyond which God's anger is kindled into a flaming fire
which devours and totally destroys.

God will protect those who take refuge in Him. But He
will woefully punish those who persistently rebel against
Him. It is therefore foolish to test God's patience and love.
Trust Him and you will be safe. Test Him and you will be
scorched!

25 SEPTEMBER

A FEARLESS FAITH—HABAKKUK
(one day to read)

". . . the just shall live by his faith" (*Habakkuk 2:4, KJV*).

Asked how she could sleep amid troubled times, an old
Christian said, "God is always watching, so there is no
point in two of us staying awake!"

At first Habakkuk didn't understand God's dealings with
Israel and the surrounding heathen nations. He was
perplexed and frustrated. But through prolonged waiting
upon God he got the answer: live by faith in the faithful
One.

His eyes still saw darkness and doom but he, by faith,
anticipated deliverance. His confidence was not in
circumstantial evidence, but in the eternal Creator and
Sustainer of the universe.

When God who never wavers is the object of your faith,
there is no need for you to waver or worry.

26 SEPTEMBER

GOD'S DAY OF JUDGMENT—ZEPHANIAH
(one day to read)

"Beg him to save you, all who are humble—all who have tried to obey. Walk humbly and do what is right; perhaps even yet the Lord will protect you from his day of wrath in that day of doom" (Zephaniah 2:3, The Living Bible).

Around the dial of a church clock in Strasbourg, France, are the words: "One of these hours the Lord is coming!" Are you ready to meet Him? God is exceedingly longsuffering, but there is a point beyond which He declares war. There is a judgment day in God's timetable, and what a dreadful day that will be!

Those who say in their hearts, "The Lord will not do good, neither will he do evil" (*1:12*), will one day find Him searching for them with lamps. And when He finds them He will strike. Zephaniah describes that dreadful day in his prophecy.

As always, there would be a remnant among God's professing people. They are the residue after God's purging fire. To remain true to God at all times, even times of fierce testing, is essential if we are to be numbered among those in whom He delights.

27 SEPTEMBER

THE FIRST, FIRST—HAGGAI
(one day to read)

"'You look for much, but behold, it comes to little; when you bring it home, I blow it away. Why?' declares the Lord of hosts, 'Because of My house which lies desolate, while each of you runs to his own house'" (Haggai 1:9).

It is wise to put first things first. Jesus said, "But seek ye first the kingdom of God, and his righteousness; and all these things [daily necessities] shall be added unto you" (*Matthew 6:33*).

The Israelites returned to their fatherland after seventy years in captivity. The building of God's temple became their first order of business. This work, however, was opposed and brought to a standstill. With nothing to do they got involved in building their own homes.

When God saw that they had become more concerned about their own homes than about His temple He allowed hard times to come their way. And not until they heeded Haggai's challenge to reexamine their priorities and again put first things first did the blessing of God return upon them.

28 SEPTEMBER

A PROPELLING PROMISE—ZECHARIAH
(three days to read)

"And the Lord will be king over all the earth; in that day the Lord will be the only one, and His name the only one" (Zechariah 14:9).

Zechariah, like Haggai, was used of God to encourage the Israelites to get on with the building of the temple until it was finished. From what he said we can learn that when God gives us a job to do, no matter how insignificant it might seem to us we are to do it heartily as unto the Lord. He pledges His own support. And any work in which God is engaged is a great work.

Learn also that when you get bogged down, you should trust in His promises for blessing. When you get discouraged, trust in His promises for deliverance. When you get hurt, trust in His promises for healing. He has a promise suited for your every need. Find it. Put faith in God to fulfill it. And you will be propelled on your way to victory.

29 SEPTEMBER

"And one called out to another and said, 'Holy, Holy, Holy, is the Lord of hosts, the whole earth is full of His glory'" (Isaiah 6:3).

There is in this doxology a prophetic challenge: we are to be instruments through which God is glorified throughout the whole earth. God is glorified when we bear much fruit (*John 15:8*). This could be considered as referring to the fruit of the Spirit or Christlike character. Or it might refer to the multiplication of disciples through the witness of believers. He is also glorified when we pray properly and He answers our prayers (*John 14:13*).

Think of God's glory being His manifested holiness, while on the other hand His holiness is His glory hidden or veiled. The ultimate objective of what God does and what His children are to do is that His holiness might become universally seen and known as His glory fills the whole earth. I must constantly evaluate what I'm doing by asking if it is contributing to that objective.

30 SEPTEMBER

"And he carried me away in the Spirit to a great and high mountain, and showed me the holy city, Jerusalem, coming down out of heaven from God" (Revelation 21:10).

The description of the holy city and of the new heaven and new earth in the book of Revelation is startling. Brilliance and grandeur such as staggers the mind are presented in the description. The distinguishing characteristic of the holy city is that "no temple could be seen in the city, for the Lord God Almighty and the Lamb are worshiped in it everywhere. And the city has no need of sun or moon to light it, for the glory of God and of the Lamb illuminate it" (*Revelation 21:22, 23, The Living Bible*).

John also points out that "nothing evil will be permitted in it—no one immoral or dishonest—but only those whose names are written in the Lamb's Book of Life" (*Revelation 21:27, The Living Bible*). And a special blessing is pronounced upon those "who are washing their robes, to have the right to enter in through the gates of the city" (*Revelation 22:14, The Living Bible*).

What a glorious eternity awaits those who through faith in Christ are ready to meet Him. What a tragedy awaits those who are not ready for that day, those who can look forward only to eternal doom. May we who know the Lord seek to share with everyone the way in which they can enter into this same blessed hope.

1 OCTOBER

THE FUTURE FOCUS—MALACHI
(one day to read)

"'Listen: I will send my messenger before me to prepare the way. And then the one you are looking for will come suddenly to his Temple—the Messenger of God's promises, to bring you great joy. Yes, he is surely coming,' says the Lord of Hosts. 'But who can live when he appears? Who can endure his coming? For he is like a blazing fire refining precious metal and he can bleach the dirtiest garments'" (Malachi 3:1, 2, The Living Bible).

> Only one life, 'twill soon be past;
> Only what's done for Christ will last.

Everything we do, therefore, should be done with an awareness that we will have to give an accounting of it in the future. This is true of our worship of God as well as of our work for God. Both must be of the highest quality.

Malachi also points out that the quality of our giving is as important as the quality of our living. The two are inseparable. The Lord said we should bring all we have that is His into His storehouse. When we do, He will richly repay.

You can never prepare too well for the future. God, however, only expects you to keep on doing your best, by His enabling.

2 OCTOBER

CHRIST THE KING ABOVE US—
MATTHEW (seven days to read)

"Come to me and I will give you rest—all of you who work so hard beneath a heavy yoke. Wear my yoke—for it fits perfectly—and let me teach you; for I am gentle and humble, and you shall find rest for your souls; for I give

you only light burdens" (Matthew 11:28-30, The Living Bible).

It isn't the way it used to be for kings. Today few of them really reign with authority. Most are just government figureheads rather than functioning heads.

Jesus Christ, our King, has the authority to reign in His kingdom. He demands submission and obedience from His subjects. As you read Matthew, you will discover the laws of His kingdom. The glorious miracles He performs confirm His claim to sovereignty. As King, He stands as the final Judge of the good and the bad. He is answerable to no one. He stands above all and has authority over all, both material and spiritual.

As King, He invites us to become His subjects. The only requirements for citizenship are that we come to Him as we are and subject ourselves to His rule. He will provide for our every need and enlist us in the great task of representing Him to the whole world.

Dr. A. W. Tozer likened Christ's present position in the Church to that of a king in a limited, constitutional monarchy. Let us initiate a change by acclaiming Him the undisputed King who rules over us fully, with our active consent.

3 OCTOBER

"The fear of the Lord is the beginning of wisdom, and the knowledge of the Holy One is understanding" (Proverbs 9:10).

"One of the most widely used terms for Deity in ancient times is *El*, with its derivations *Elim*, *Elohim*, and *Eloah*. But like the Greek *theos*, the Latin *Deus*, and the English *God*, it is a generic name, including every other member of the class deity. It expresses majesty and authority, although the meaning of the root *El* is lost in obscurity. Gesenius took it to be a part of the verb *to be strong*, and so the

Strong One; Noeldeke connected it with the Arabic root for *to be in front,* and so the Governor or Leader; Dillman traced it to a root with the sense of power or might; Legarde sought its explanation in a root which made it mean *the goal.* The plural *Elohim* is used regularly by the Old Testament writers with singular verbs and adjectives to denote a singular idea."[28]

This plural name is used in Genesis 1:1, suggesting the first reference to the Trinity found in the Bible. It was the Triune God who spoke the world and the heavens into existence.

4 OCTOBER

"In the beginning God [Elohim] created the heavens and the earth" (Genesis 1:1).

A professor under whom I once studied pointed out, "The etymology of the word *Elohim* seems to come from two meanings of the word *Eloah.* One has the meaning to reverence or worship or adore. According to this meaning God is placed before us from the very beginning as the only true object of our worship. As our Creator He has the right to demand our allegiance.

"The other meaning . . . is 'to swear as an oath.' This gives us the Trinity as engaged in an eternal covenant. This is the covenant keeping God. It shows that with an oath the three members of the Holy Trinity, back from an eternity, entered into covenant as regards the creation and redemption of man. We read of Christ as constituted a priest forever after the order of Melchizedek by an oath. We read of the 'blood of the everlasting covenant.' We read that Christ was the lamb slain before the foundation of the world. So the full meaning would seem to be the Trinity as the only object of man's adoration and worship in covenant for

28. *Op. cit., Thiessen, p. 52.*

man's redemption. In its various forms this name for God is used some 2,600 times in the Old Testament" (Bragg).

5 OCTOBER

"And he blessed him and said, 'Blessed be Abram of God Most High [El Elyon], possessor of heaven and earth; and blessed be God Most High, who has delivered your enemies into your hand.' And he gave him a tenth of all" (Genesis 14:19, 20).

It would be humbling to realize that one's efforts toward a good cause were blessed by God Most High. That title not only identifies Him as the only true God, it declares Him to be in a position elevated over all other beings and things. As the Most High, God "gave the nations their inheritance . . . He set the boundaries" (*Deuteronomy 32:8*).

Daniel solemnly informed Nebuchadnezzar that he must recognize "that the Most High is ruler over the realm of mankind, and bestows it on whomever He wishes" (*Daniel 4:25*). Nebuchadnezzar, after resisting Daniel's counsel and suffering severe consequences, finally came to realize that the Most High was not just free to do as He chose in the realm of earth, but also in heaven above (*Daniel 4:35-37*). Man is a fool not to reverence and obey *El Elyon*, the Most High God.

6 OCTOBER

"I am God Almighty [El Shaddai]; walk before Me, and be blameless. And I will establish My covenant between Me and you" (Genesis 17:1, 2).

This is the first time God reveals Himself as *El Shaddai*,

The Almighty. He had previously established a covenant of blessing with Abraham, but thus far the most important part of the covenant remained unfulfilled. And the possibility of its being fulfilled was diminishing every passing day. Abraham's body at ninety-nine years of age was nearly dead insofar as reproducing powers were concerned, and Sarah's womb was now definitely dead.

But with the God who is Almighty what are such minor hindrances? Abraham was told to walk before God in a blameless way—that would include trusting God for the fulfillment of His promise. If Abraham kept himself in the place and posture where God could bless him, God the Almighty would in His time do His part. *El Shaddai* always does.

7 OCTOBER

"I am Almighty God [El Shaddai]"
(Genesis 17:1).

Scofield has some further thoughts on this name of God. "(1) . . . The qualifying word *Shaddai* is formed from the Hebrew word *shad*, the breast, invariably used in Scripture for a woman's breast . . . *Shaddai* therefore means primarily 'the breasted.' God is '*Shaddai*,' because He is the Nourisher, the Strength-giver, and so, in a secondary sense, the Satisfier, who pours Himself into believing lives. As a fretful, unsatisfied babe is not only strengthened and nourished from the mother's breast, but also is quieted, rested, satisfied, so *El Shaddai* is that name of God which sets Him forth as the Strength-giver and Satisfier of His people . . . 'All-sufficient' would far better express both the Hebrew meaning and the characteristic use of the name in Scripture.

"(2) Almighty God (*El Shaddai*) not only enriches, but makes *fruitful*. This is nowhere better illustrated than in the first occurrence of the name (*Genesis 17:1-8*) . . . To the same purport is the use of the name in Genesis 28:3, 4.

"(3) As Giver of fruitfulness, Almighty God (*El Shaddai*) chastens His people. For the moral connection of chastening with fruit-bearing, see John 15:2; Hebrews 12:10; Ruth 1:20. Hence, Almighty is the characteristic name of God in Job, occurring thirty-one times in that book. The hand of *El Shaddai* falls upon Job, the best man of his time, not in *judgment,* but in purifying unto greater fruitfulness (*Job 5:17-25*)."[29]

8 OCTOBER

"And Abraham planted a tamarisk tree at Beersheba, and there he called on the name of the Lord, the Everlasting God [El Olam]" (Genesis 21:33).

There had been a dispute between Abraham and Abimelech which they now had settled. They made a covenant of peace. After Abimelech left, Abraham planted this tamarisk tree. Why? This type of tree, with its hard wood and its long, narrow, thickly clustered, evergreen leaves, generally had an exceptionally long life. Abraham was no doubt saying to the Lord, whom he here addresses as *El Olam*, the Everlasting God, "May this tree be a long-lasting reminder that You, the Everlasting God, will keep an eye on Abimelech and me concerning this covenant of peace we have established." The name *El Olam* does not signify only God's eternity, but that He oversees to the end the way in which agreements are carried out.

29. *From The Scofield Reference Bible. Copyright © 1917, renewed 1945 by Oxford University Press, New York. Reprinted by permission, p. 26.*

9 OCTOBER

CHRIST THE COMMANDER BEFORE US—
MARK (five days to read)

"And Jesus said to them, 'Follow Me, and I will make you become fishers of men'" (Mark 1:17).

General Dwight Eisenhower committed the Allied forces to the Normandy mission in World War 2 when he uttered the fateful words, "Okay, let's go!"

In reading Mark you will discover Christ as the Commander before us calling out, "Let's go!" The commander's job is to lead his subordinates in fulfilling his superior's orders. He is a servant and a master at the same time.

As a servant, Christ had orders from above. According to Mark He never disobeyed. Note the many occurrences of the word *Straightway*, characterizing a faithful servant.

As the Master, Christ enlists you to participate in the job He came into the world to do. His life presents a pattern to follow. He was a faithful servant and He demands that you follow in His footsteps. The privilege is yours, but so is the responsibility. Stand therefore behind your great Commander and let Him lead you on to victory.

10 OCTOBER

"I am Jehovah, the Almighty God who appeared to Abraham, Isaac, and Jacob— though I did not reveal my name, Jehovah, to them" (Exodus 6:2, 3, The Living Bible).

The word we translate as *Jehovah* is a form of the Hebrew verb *to be*. When Moses asked how he should identify God when talking to others about Him, God said, "I am who I am" *(Exodus 3:14)*. Some would say this could be translated, "I am, I am being." God is always all that we need—our Savior, our Protector and Provider, and our Father. He is, as Manford Gutzke says, our Eternal Contemporary.

This name points to the uniqueness of God, who is infinite, eternal, and unconditioned. He is the only true existence in the universe. Everything else that is has a *derived* existence. He alone is underived, self-existent, and complete within Himself.

11 OCTOBER

"And Abraham called the name of that place The Lord Will Provide [Jehovah-Jireh], as it is said to this day, 'In the mount of the Lord it will be provided'" (Genesis 22:14).

Abraham had often stepped out by faith to do something God asked him to do. And without exception God faithfully provided what was necessary for him to carry out the mission. Any promises God made were always fulfilled. There were other times, however, when Abraham did not step out by faith in obedience. Even in those cases God remained faithful to him.

The most notable incident was when Abraham had Ishmael by Hagar rather than waiting to have a son by Sarah, which God had promised to provide. Even in that instance of Abraham's disbelief, God provided what He had promised.

When Isaac, the promised son, had grown to be a young man, God asked Abraham to sacrifice him up to the Lord, by faith. By that time Abraham had come to realize that God would remain faithful and would "provide for Himself the lamb for the burnt offering" (*Genesis 22:8*). With that confidence, obedience was Abraham's difficult but faithful response. The drama moves to a climax when God at the last moment stops Abraham from killing his son. And at that precise moment God also supplies a ram caught nearby in a thicket by his horns. That ram was just what Abraham needed to culminate his sacrificial offering of praise to the Lord.

Was it coincidental that the timing worked out as it did? No! *Jehovah-Jireh*, the Lord Will Provide, was behind it all, revealing Himself as the faithful provider of all that His people need to obey Him.

12 OCTOBER

"I will put none of the diseases on you which I have put on the Egyptians; for I, the Lord (Jehovah-Rapha), am your healer" (Exodus 15:26).

God uses rather unique ways to teach us at times. Here He led Israel, which was wandering through the wilderness, to some water. Coming to the water with high expectation, the Israelites were understandably distressed when they discovered it was bitter. Their immediate response was to grumble at Moses. Moses in turn cried to the Lord who instructed him to take a tree and throw it into the water. And to the amazement of all, the waters then became sweet.

Why would God go through this process? First, to test them (v. 25). Through the test it became obvious that they still had not learned to trust in God. In fact, they failed doubly by grumbling. Then, by providing a solution God taught them again that He could be trusted in every situation. Finally, and most important, He revealed Himself as their great Physician. Egypt experienced many diseases as judgment for their rebellion. God promised that none of those diseases would inflict the Israelites if they walked rightly before Him. He would be their Healer, *Jehovah-Rapha*.

13 OCTOBER

"And Moses built an altar, and named it The Lord [Jehovah-Nissi] is My Banner"
(Exodus 17:15).

Fierce opposition confronts us at times. Left to ourselves we could not stand in the face of such opposition. But as the people of God we have the privilege of prayer which puts us in contact with an all-sufficient source of assistance.

Moses recognized the need for God's intervention in the battle between Israel and the Amalekites. He sent out his best troops under the able leadership of Joshua, and promised to give himself to prayer support. When he held his hands up to God as an expression of his desire for God's involvement, the battle went well for Israel. When he relented because of tiredness and dropped his hands, the battle turned in favor of Amalek. God gave wisdom to Moses, and he devised a way to prevail in prayer. God responded by giving a total victory.

As a memorial Moses built an altar and worshiped God as the One who leads His forces into victory. God—*Jehovah-Nissi*—is our banner too. He will not fail us when we put ourselves in a relationship by which He can work in us and through us. Prayer puts us in that place.

14 OCTOBER

CHRIST THE COMPANION BESIDE US—
LUKE (eight days to read)
"As they walked along they were talking of Jesus' death, when suddenly Jesus himself came along and joined them and began walking beside them" (Luke 24:14, 15, The Living Bible).

Are you one of the lonely crowd we hear so much about these days? Are you without a real friend? If so, be alert as you read Luke's Gospel. You'll be introduced to Christ the companion.

A true companion is one who walks and talks with us. He is one who comes alongside to help us triumph when alone we would tremble and fall.

Throughout the book, Christ chose for Himself the title, "The Son of Man." He said, "The Son of Man is come to seek and to save that which was lost" (*Luke 19:10*). He had to become a man in order to save men. But as a man He did far more than that. He showed sympathy for the weak, the suffering, and the outcast. And He did something about their condition.

Jesus Christ was always available to help. And He still is. So why not ask Him in prayer to enter your life and go with you day by day as your companion.

15 OCTOBER

"Then Gideon built an altar there to the Lord and named it The Lord is Peace [Jehovah-Shalom]" (*Judges 6:24*).

In the thick of a battle we sometimes feel forsaken by God. When nothing seems to go our way, defeat seems almost certain. Should we let such circumstances cause us to give up? No. Look at Gideon, who in the face of Israel's imminent danger of attack from Midian, beat out wheat in the winepress. He kept busy doing what seemed best to preserve himself.

God honored Gideon's diligence with a visitation by the angel of the Lord. Overwhelmed by this experience, Gideon feared the consequences of seeing the angel of the Lord face

to face. "'It's all right,' the Lord replied. 'Don't be afraid!
You shall not die'" (*Judges 6:23, The Living Bible*). God
was promising him not only peace with Himself, but also
peace as a nation by helping Gideon's warriors defeat their
enemies.

God delights in giving His children His peace to rule in
their hearts (*Colossians 3:15*), and keeping them in Christ
Jesus (*Philippians 4:7*). Seek the Lord in your time of
testing until you find Him as *Jehovah-Shalom*.

16 OCTOBER

*"And this is His name by which He will be
called, 'The Lord our Righteousness' [Jehovah-
Tsidkenu]"* (*Jeremiah 23:6*).

God's concern for His sheep is here further amplified by a
promise of restoration. Unfaithful leaders had led the people
into what would become their captivity. There would be a
tendency on the part of the people of God to blame Him.
They needed to be reminded that God is always righteous in
what He does, whether with the ungodly or with His own.

God had made promises before. He was not going to
renege on those promises. Neither was He going to fulfill
them without first dealing righteously with His unrighteous
and unfaithful people. God cannot condone sin, even in
those He loves.

Today, in our world, God is often called unrighteous for
what He allows to happen in individual lives as well as in
the world at large. But in a coming day we will know
better. Then every knee shall bow and every tongue declare,
"The Lord is righteous." And for those who know Him
through faith, the confession will be more personal: "The
Lord *Our* Righteousness."

17 OCTOBER

*"The name of the city from that day shall be,
'The Lord is there' [Jehovah-Shammah]"*
(*Ezekiel 48:35*).

At Christ's birth He was given the name *Immanuel*,
which meant "God is with us" (*Matthew 1:23, The Living
Bible*). When He ascended to heaven after His sacrificial
work, He sent the Holy Spirit to dwell in the midst of His
people (*1 Corinthians 3:16*). A day is coming when He will
return to earth to establish His kingdom in Jerusalem, from
which center He will rule the whole world in peace.
Jehovah's presence in Jerusalem will be that city's crowning
glory. Nothing compares with an awareness of the Lord's
presence. Greater comfort can be found nowhere else.

Ezekiel's vision is of the city during the millennial age.
The apostle John in Revelation saw it as the eternal city.
No doubt the temporal kingdom will in some way merge
into the eternal, for the glorious promise concerning
Jerusalem's future state is found in its name, *Jehovah-
Shammah,* "the Lord is there."

18 OCTOBER

*"How lovely are Thy dwelling places, O Lord
of hosts [Jehovah-Tsebaoth]"* (*Psalm 84:1*).

The Lord is omnipresent and omnipotent. Nothing is
higher than Him. He is over all. All is subject to Him. In
this Psalm He is worshiped and extolled as the one over all
the hosts of heaven, all of whom are concerned about
serving, honoring, and glorifying Him. Their constant
declaration is, "Holy, Holy, Holy is the Lord God."

Adoring the Lord, basking in His presence, responding to
His every beck and call, giving Him undivided attention—
that is the atmosphere of heaven. The Psalmist declares,
"How lovely are Thy dwelling places." This is the place of

perfect rest. All who are His have this to look forward to. And to prepare themselves they should discipline themselves to enter into these spiritual dimensions of worship now. Our prayer should genuinely be, "May your will be done here on earth, just as it is in heaven" (*Matthew 6:10, The Living Bible*).

19 OCTOBER

*"The Lord is my shepherd [Jehovah-Raah],
I shall not want" (Psalm 23:1).*

This name of God communicates so many ideas of what God is in His dealings with man. He owns His flock, and His flock know Him. He has an attachment to His flock beyond their value—He is willing to lay down His life for His flock. He guides them, protects them, provides for them, and punishes them—all according to their need. To summarize, He cares for His flock.

That is why the Psalmist declares, "I shall not want." I can remember a warm, elderly Christian man in Jamaica telling of a little girl who was saying the 23rd Psalm in her church. She started, "The Lord is my Shepherd, He's all I want." Though misquoting the Psalmist, she caught the essence of the shepherd image. In Him you have all you need.

20 OCTOBER

"For you were continually straying like sheep, but now you have returned to the Shepherd and Guardian of your soul" (1 Peter 2:25).

Jesus Christ, who "personally carried the load of our sins in his own body when he died on the cross" (*1 Peter 2:24, The Living Bible*), is *Jehovah-Raah* of the Old Testament. He is the one who cares for us by doing all that is necessary not only to bring us, His straying sheep, back into His fold, but also to protect us as our constant guardian or overseer.

It is Jesus Christ, the Shepherd, who guarantees the security and safety of His sheep. He protects them from thieves who would break in and steal, and from wolves that would devour them. No one is able to pluck His sheep out of His hands. Furthermore, no one is able to pluck them out of His Father's hands. His sheep are secure in Him (*John 10:1-30*).

21 OCTOBER

"When the Chief Shepherd appears"
(*1 Peter 5:4*).

Jesus Christ, the New Testament *Jehovah-Raah*, is here referred to as the Chief Shepherd. He stands peerless, alone, above all others as the one who cares for His own. At times it seems as though He is not doing His job as our Shepherd, but we don't need to have all our problems resolved *now*, because our Chief Shepherd will appear at the appointed time to set things straight. He "is able to keep you from stumbling, and to make you stand in the presence of His glory blameless with great joy" (*Jude 24*). Even if you are one out of a hundred who for some reason has gone astray and is lost, He will seek you out until He finds you and has you back, safe in the fold (*Luke 15:3-7*). He will never fail you.

22 OCTOBER

CHRIST THE CREATOR WITHIN US—
JOHN (seven days to read)

"I am the vine, you are the branches; he who abides in Me, and I in him, he bears much fruit; for apart from Me you can do nothing" (*John 15:5*).

When certain Egyptian tombs were opened some years ago, researchers discovered wheat in them. For 4,000 years that wheat had remained in the dry darkness of those tombs. When it was brought out and planted, it grew and produced a crop. All it needed was to be put into proper relationship with the earth, the air, and the sun.

As you read John, note carefully the evidence which points to the fact that Jesus Christ is God. Then consider that as soil must receive the grain of wheat before the seed brings forth new life, so you must receive Jesus Christ into your life by faith before He will bring forth new life in and through you.

Jesus Christ came to bring into your experience abundant life (*John 10:10*). Today, bow in prayer and ask Him to fulfill that purpose in your life. He will not disappoint you.

23 OCTOBER

"For today in the city of David there has been born for you a Savior, who is Christ the Lord" (*Luke 2:11*).

The title Christ comes from the Greek word *Christos*, which means *anointed*. In a ceremony a person appointed to a specific task was anointed by having oil poured on his head. Christ was anointed by His Father when at His baptism the Holy Spirit descended upon Him in the form of a dove.

The Hebrew equivalent for this title is *Messiah.* These titles are similar to the Latin *Caesar,* the German *Kaiser,* the Russian *Czar,* and the Persian *Shah.* All these titles indicate that the person bearing the title has been selected and installed in a special, important office.

Throughout the Old Testament God promised to send His people a special Messiah to bring them salvation. The New Testament declares Jesus of Nazareth to be the One God selected for and anointed to do this special work. New Testament writers wanted their readers to discover and trust in Jesus as "the Christ, the Son of God; and that believing you may have life in His name" *(John 20:31).*

24 OCTOBER

"And she will bear a Son; and you shall call His name Jesus, for it is He who will save His people from their sins" (Matthew 1:21).

It may surprise you that the name *Jesus* was in common use for boys of the first century—much as Tom or Bob or Bill are used today. To some people even now, the name *Jesus* merely represents the human form of the One who is in reality the Savior of the world. But when true Christians use the name, they are referring to the unique human being born in Bethlehem, who grew up in a little village called Nazareth.

This name *Jesus* is the Greek equivalent of the Hebrew name *Joshua. Joshua* means "God is my Savior" or "Jehovah is my salvation." This is why Joseph and Mary were instructed to give the name to the child born to them. He was to save His people from their sins. Freely translated, *Jesus* means "God is my salvation."

When you put the name and the title together—as *Jesus Christ* or as *Christ Jesus*—you have: "My salvation is found in the promised anointed One."

25 OCTOBER

"Listen! The virgin shall conceive a child! She shall give birth to a Son, and he shall be called 'Emmanuel' (meaning 'God is with us')" (Matthew 1:23, The Living Bible).

There probably is no greater truth than the one communicated in the name *Immanuel* or *Emmanuel*, which means, "God with us." This name given to Jesus Christ at His birth declares emphatically that He is God. It also points out that the God who is out there has come to where we are. He has visited mankind. And it promises His presence with us.

Jesus said, "I will never, *never* fail you nor forsake you" (*Hebrews 13:5, The Living Bible*). In the final words of his first epistle John writes, "We know that Christ, God's Son has come" (*1 John 5:20, The Living Bible*). This declaration of John is comforting to the Christian. *Has come* includes *has arrived* and *is present*. In the incarnation Jesus Christ came, arrived among men. He did bodily depart after His resurrection, but the Bible informs us over and over again that He is also present in His Church and in each individual believer. *Immanuel* has come. He is present with us, never to leave us!

26 OCTOBER

"For the Son of Man has come to seek and to save that which was lost" (Luke 19:10).

Over eighty times the New Testament identifies Jesus Christ as the Son of Man. This name for Jesus Christ refers to His being human. A mortal body was prepared for Him. In the incarnation He entered that body. In that body He experienced all that we experience, so it could be said of Him, "For we do not have a high priest who cannot sympathize with our weaknesses, but one who has been tempted in all things as we are, yet without sin" (*Hebrews 4:15*). By being baptized Jesus emphasized His identification with sinful man (*Matthew 3:15*).

As man He was able to be man's substitute in taking upon Himself the sin of mankind and paying its dreadful penalty. He died physically, as the Son of Man, for our sins. He was buried physically. And He was raised physically from among the dead. He is the first fruits of those who, having believed, will be raised from among the dead (*1 Corinthians 15:23*). He is now the glorified Son of Man at the Father's right hand (*Acts 7:56*).

27 OCTOBER

"For the Son of Man is going to come in the glory of His Father with His angels" (*Matthew 16:27*).

The title *Son of Man* does not focus only on Jesus Christ's humanity. Some passages speak of the Son of Man in heaven and of His coming in the glory of His Father. "And then they shall see the Son of Man coming in clouds with great power and glory" (*Mark 13:26*). A third group of Scriptures refer to the suffering of the Son of Man. "And He began to teach them that the Son of Man must suffer many things and be rejected by the elders and the chief priests and the scribes, and be killed, and after three days rise again" (*Mark 8:31*).

Though all three emphases concerning the Son of Man are found, the primary emphasis should focus on His sovereignty, His authority, and His deity (*Daniel 7:13, 14*). Though fully identifying with us as man, Jesus always remained God.

28 OCTOBER

"He said, 'I am the Son of God'"
(Matthew 27:43).

Jesus used this designation to declare His origin. He always was, is, and always will be the Son of God. He became the son of Adam at a point in history. When using the word *son* we automatically think of *father*. They belong together. In a unique way Jesus and the Father are eternally one (*John 10:30*).

At Christ's baptism a voice from heaven said, "This is my beloved Son, and I am wonderfully pleased with him" (*Matthew 3:17, The Living Bible*). Again at His transfiguration, a voice solemnly declared, "This is my beloved Son, and I am wonderfully pleased with him. Obey him" (*Matthew 17:5, The Living Bible*). When Philip asked Jesus to show him the Father, Jesus replied, "Anyone who has seen me has seen the Father" (*John 14:9, The Living Bible*).

God did not choose a man and endow him with qualities of character that made him a better man than all others. No, He sent His eternal Son to take upon Himself the form of man to fulfill His Father's will. The Son of God is God the Son.

29 OCTOBER

CHRIST THE CHURCH-BUILDER
THROUGH US—ACTS (ten days to read)

"But you shall receive power when the Holy Spirit has come upon you; and you shall be My witnesses both in

Jerusalem, and in all Judea and Samaria, and even to the remotest part of the earth" (Acts 1:8).

Christ's great mission is to seek and to save that which was lost. When one who was lost is saved, he becomes a member of Christ's Church. In Acts you will find out how this process began and continued until representation from all parts of the first-century world were a part of the Church.

You also will discover that Jesus Christ used anyone— man, woman, or young person—who made himself available to the Holy Spirit for service. And you will find that the secret of success in this development was that the Church took her witness out into the world where the lost were to be found.

The Church today must rediscover that Jesus Christ is not looking for ability, nor inability, as much as He is looking for availability. We must also realize anew that C. E. Autrey is right in urging us to give the Church a chance to breathe by going outside.

30 OCTOBER

"Through Him then let us continually offer up a sacrifice of praise to God, that is, the fruit of lips that give thanks to His name" (Hebrews 13:15).

Praise is the highest exercise of faith. It acknowledges the source of every good and perfect gift. When offered in advance, it conveys the thrill of anticipation. And it is the most positive perspective you can have when facing a trial or a challenge.

Praise is often spontaneous, prompted by an obvious act of God in blessing. It is to be expressed, however, even when things don't turn out as desired. That's when it becomes "a sacrifice of praise to God." Some have said, "In the future time all sacrifices shall cease; but praises shall not cease."

God declares that at certain times if we humans didn't praise the Lord, even the stones would cry out (*Luke 19:40*). The Psalmist invokes heaven and earth to praise Him—"the seas and everything that moves in them" (*Psalm 69:34*).

Indeed, "the Lord is beyond description, and greatly to be praised" (*Psalm 96:4, The Living Bible*).

31 OCTOBER

"Shout joyfully to the Lord . . . serve the Lord with gladness, come before Him with joyful singing" (Psalm 100:1).

"Give hilariously to the Lord!" I'll never forget that admonition by Dr. Alan Redpath as he took up an offering in a conference some years ago. It seemed rather odd to me at that time. Over the years I have come to understand that what he said was biblical. Too much of our giving and living is done grudgingly and out of necessity, rather than out of the abundance of our heart.

The Psalmist captures the same spirit of worship and service as a child of God. He is not describing an irrational, emotional high. He gives reasons for praise and thanksgiving. Knowing who God is (v. 3) and what He is like (v. 5), as well as who we are as His children (v. 3), is sufficient grounds for us to break forth at any time with singing and praise.

It is this quality of life that makes Christianity contagious. Begin the day with praise and then, throughout the day, in everything give thanks (*1 Thessalonians 5:18*). Ask God to fill you with His Spirit and to give you a new, joyful song in all that you do (*Ephesians 5:18, 19*). Praise is powerful.

1 NOVEMBER

"Joseph . . . called Barnabas by the apostles (which translated means, Son of Encouragement)" (Acts 4:36).

It is not enough merely to learn truth about the Bible. Nor is it enough merely to read the Bible. To hide its truth in our hearts we must *study* the Bible.

One method of study which is highly profitable is the biographical. In this approach you try to picture the life of a person as revealed in the Bible in order to learn from his example. As you read Acts you will encounter Barnabas. List all the things you find mentioned about him.

For example, take Acts 4:36. There you find that Barnabas was a Hebrew of the tribe of Levi. He was born in Cyprus. The apostles called him Barnabas. Why? Because he always encouraged, exhorted, or consoled those around him. As you study his life you will see this very evident. Put down all the facts you find about him after each reference you find about him in your reading. You will find him referred to in chapters 9, 11, 12, 13, 14, and 15.

2 NOVEMBER

"Even Barnabas was carried away by their hypocrisy" (Galatians 2:13).

Not much is said about Barnabas outside of the book of Acts. This chapter in Galatians, however, shows us that Barnabas with all of his great qualities also exhibited weakness at times. Here religious and social pressure was quite strong. Even though he had received the blessing of the pillars of the church in Jerusalem to go with Paul to reach the Gentiles, he deferred to the Jews, to Paul's dismay.

We find in other books that Barnabas' nephew and

protégé, Mark, finally emerged as a mature, useful servant of God. Barnabas passed into oblivion after he took Mark under his wing. But Mark, for whom he made this sacrifice, rewarded Barnabas with fruitful years of service with both Peter and Paul. And he became the author of the Gospel which bears his name.

3 NOVEMBER

"They were all afraid of him . . . but Barnabas took hold of him and brought him to the apostles" (Acts 9:27).

Once you have gathered all the information you can from the Bible's references to a person, then it's helpful to organize these facts. You can organize them chronologically and develop a historical sketch. Or you can develop a character sketch.

Following is an example of a historical sketch of Barnabas.

Introduction: a Levite, born in Cyprus
  I. His life in the Jerusalem church
    1. A landowner
    2. Sold all he had and gave all to the church
    3. Sent to examine the spread of gospel in Antioch
 II. His life with Paul
    1. Secures him in the fellowship of the church
    2. Enlists him in the work of God
    3. Pushes him to the fore in the missionary team
    4. Has a sharp disagreement with him and separates
III. His life with Mark
    1. His uncle
    2. Disappointed in Mark's departure
    3. Gives him another opportunity
    4. Reproduces his faith in Mark

4 NOVEMBER

"Barnabas . . . rejoiced and began to encourage them all . . . for he was a good man, and full of the Holy Spirit and of faith" (Acts 11:22-24).

Wherever Barnabas went, whether in a crowd or with one person, he encouraged one and all. His very presence was an encouragement. He used the Word of God to teach—this was the basis of his encouragement. He recognized his own limitations and others' potential. He enlisted others to exercise their gifts, and as they became more proficient he would thrust them into leadership and look for someone else to encourage.

Barnabas was self-effacing in his ministry of building others. Perhaps he taught Paul the principle of 2 Timothy 2:2. He was not out for his own recognition. If anyone was to get recognition he was content to let others have it. But he was a man of resolute heart who would stand on principle or conviction. Oh, that God would raise up more men like Barnabas!

5 NOVEMBER

"A crowd began to gather and soon the city was filled with confusion. Everyone rushed to the amphitheater, dragging along Gaius and Aristarchus, Paul's traveling companions, for trial" (Acts 19:29, The Living Bible).

Paul learned from Barnabas the importance of multiplying his ministry by reproducing his faith in others. He had a traveling Bible school as he went from city to city. They learned firsthand the challenge of the gospel. Gaius, referred to only in four places in the Bible, was one of the team. You find Gaius in this reference and in Acts 20:4; Romans 16:23; 1 Corinthians 1:14. Look up each of these references and put down all the facts you can find about Gaius. You might have to read a few verses before and after each reference to get the context of each statement.

6 NOVEMBER

"Gaius, host to me and to the whole church, greets you" (Romans 16:23).

Now that you have the facts about Gaius down, sort them out and develop a sketch of his life. Obviously it will be but a fragment in comparison to what might be done with some who are mentioned more often, like Paul or Timothy, but it will give you exercise in developing this Bible study skill.

Gaius was from Derbe. He was no doubt reached for Christ during Paul's first missionary trip. He was one of the few baptized by Paul. There is an indication that he moved and finally located in Rome. He evidently traveled with Paul for a time and then settled down to a more permanent ministry, with the church meeting in his home. He was a weathered soldier of the cross.

7 NOVEMBER

"He was accompanied by . . . Gaius" (Acts 20:4).

Even from this rather limited exposure to Gaius you see things about him that you can apply to your own life. First, he went beyond mere faith and baptism; he was willing to go forth in service. Second, he did not cop out when his service to God involved suffering. Third, what was his he made available to others in the family of God. Not only did he open his home for the church to meet in, he also opened

it to individual believers who needed a place to stay. Do you
have that kind of commitment?

The biographical study method is very beneficial. Use it
often for your own personal enrichment.

8 NOVEMBER

ABUNDANT LIVING—ROMANS
(six days to read)

*"I urge you therefore, brethren, by the mercies of God, to
present your bodies a living and holy sacrifice, acceptable to
God, which is your spiritual service of worship. And do not
be conformed to this world, but be transformed by the
renewing of your mind, that you may prove what the will
of God is, that which is good and acceptable and perfect"*
(Romans 12:1, 2).

It was St. Augustine who long ago said, "You have made
us for Yourself, O God, and our hearts are restless till they
find their rest in You." More recently Pascal said, "There is
a God-shaped vacuum in the heart of each man which
cannot be satisfied by any created thing but only by God,
the Creator, made known through Jesus Christ."

Read Romans carefully, for it is a thorough explanation
of the Christian life. It begins with what man is apart from
God, and what he can be when he takes by faith the
provisions God has made through Jesus Christ. The most
precious of those provisions for the one trusting in Jesus
Christ is the presence and power of the Holy Spirit. When
He is given full control, He frees us from all that holds us
back and enables us to enter and do all that pleases God.
Take special note of the practical instructions for abundant
living, beginning with chapter 12.

9 NOVEMBER

"I am eager to preach the gospel to you"
(Romans 1:15).

Another Bible study method might be called the synthetic method. In this approach to study, you take a portion of Scripture or preferably a given book of the Bible, and seek to find the main theme. Then having found the main theme, you look for main points which support or amplify the theme. You can take it a step further and find subpoints which support each of the main points. As you carry this through, you essentially end up with an outline. Based upon the outline you make some deductions. These you must then relate to or apply to your life.

10 NOVEMBER

"The gospel . . . is the power of God for salvation to everyone who believes"
(Romans 1:16).

If you read Romans over a few times, you will likely come to the conclusion that the theme of the book has to do with salvation. You might state for example: "Salvation defined: past, present, and future." Paul treats the subject in a thorough, logical way, building to a climax at the end of chapter 8. Then he gives historical perspective to the subject through chapter 11. Based upon this foundation, he presents a practical challenge related to every area of a believer's life. Don't leave Romans without an understanding of what it means to have been saved, to be progressively being saved, and to anticipate your ultimate salvation. Read the book a few times to sense its main thrust.

11 NOVEMBER

*"The free gift of God is eternal life in Christ
Jesus our Lord" (Romans 6:23).*

Now that you have the main theme you will want to find
the supportive main points. Let me give you an example of
what I mean:

Chapters 1-3—The universal need for salvation
Chapters 4-6—The available provision of salvation
Chapters 7-8—The potential growth within salvation
Chapters 9-11—The historical perspective to salvation
Chapters 12-16—The practical outworking of salvation

You might have come up with some different main points.
That's fine as long as they cover the material found in each
portion under consideration.

12 NOVEMBER

*"Be transformed by the renewing of your mind,
that you may prove what the will of God is"
(Romans 12:2).*

As an example of developing the outline to include
subpoints which support the main points, let me take my
final main point: the practical outworking of salvation,
chapters 12-16.

12:1-9—How to participate in the church's ministry
12:10-21—How to relate to people in general
13—How to be a responsible citizen
14—How to overcome a judgmental attitude
15:1-13—How to love a weaker brother
15:14-33—How to win the world to Christ
16—How the extended family of believers encouraged
each other.

Now try going to your outline and developing some
supportive subpoints for each of the main points you found.

13 NOVEMBER

"Him who is able to establish you according to my gospel" (Romans 16:25).

As you develop this study in Romans you will discover that salvation past, present, and future are all out of our reach if left to ourselves. God alone is able to bring us into experiencing this three-dimensional fullness of salvation. Praise His name! There are many practical applications to be made based upon our study. A few might be:

1. The Christian's life, growth, and service are all matters of faith, not works.
2. The Christian needs others if he is to grow. Even Paul did.
3. The Christian must fulfill his civil responsibilities.
4. The Christian must not be judgmental in minor issues of conscience.

Try this type of study on other books of the Bible. You might want to cover some of the briefer books.

14 NOVEMBER

SEVER THE LEAVEN—1 CORINTHIANS
(six days to read)

"Your boasting is not good. Do you not know that a little leaven leavens the whole lump of dough? Clean out the old leaven, that you may be a new lump, just as you are in fact unleavened. For Christ our Passover also has been sacrificed" (1 Corinthians 5:6, 7).

There are no "inactive" church members. A pastor whose flock numbered 100 was asked how many active members he had. "One hundred," he replied; "fifty active for me and fifty active against me."

If what you have just read makes you chuckle and say, "That's the way it is," then you'd better read 1 Corinthians with care. Paul decries a condition where disunity and other sins are present in the church and are not disciplined. Even a little leaven will leaven the whole lump if not removed. Leaven is referred to symbolically in the Bible as that which defiles. It is evil working to make more evil. Therefore, the Christian must purge the leaven from his life if he is to succeed in living for God.

The positive aspect of Paul's answer is found in chapter 13 where he exalts love. Study that chapter until it becomes a part of your way of life.

15 NOVEMBER

"A new commandment I give to you, that you love one another, even as I have loved you" (*John 13:34*).

Early Christians were known for their love toward each other. So should we. For love is the distinguishing mark of true Christianity (*John 13:34, 35*). Jesus is an example of this love. He doesn't love us because of who we are, but in spite of who we are. When He washed His disciples' feet, He did not omit Judas, whom He knew would betray Him. At the supper He offered Judas the "sop"—customarily an expression of honor.

Billy Sunday pinpointed the essence of loving one another when he said, "Do unto others what you would have them do unto you, *only do it first.*"

Genuine love for one another within Christ's Church will not go unnoticed (*John 13:35*). It will be as obvious as two young lovers. Others will see it in our eyes. It will provoke the inquiry, "What's gotten into you lately?" And its magnetic power will draw men and women to enquire into and discover the source of real love, Jesus Christ.

16 NOVEMBER

*"Being diligent to preserve the unity of the
Spirit in the bond of peace" (Ephesians 4:3).*

When we know peace in our hearts with God, then we
are to do what we can to live at peace with one another,
especially within the Church. Jesus Christ prayed for
oneness or harmony within the Church (*John 17:21, 22*). To
accomplish this objective requires humility and gentleness,
patience and forbearance with one another, and love
(*Ephesians 4:2*). If we think we are more important than
others, we will promote competition and conflict.

If we are not willing to allow God the necessary time to
do His work in the lives of others, we will provoke discord
and frustration. Some require gentle treatment and others
require extensive forbearance because of inherent limiting
factors. We will be more patient and believing in our work
with others if we recognize that God is deeply concerned
with the ongoing growth of the corporate Church and of
each individual member. Remember, God loves them too.
You will find some who are hard to get along with. Paul
says, "Be at peace with everyone, just as much as possible"
(*Romans 12:18, The Living Bible*). Try never to be the
reason for discord among believers.

17 NOVEMBER

"Let love be without hypocrisy" (Romans 12:9).

It is easy to love some people in sincerity. To
love others is difficult. Knowing that we are to love even
our enemies might prompt us to act out, simulate, play out
the part, pretend that we love them. In reality our
expressions in such a case are sheer hypocrisy.

How do you resolve such a predicament? Love by faith.

You know God loves the person. You know the fruit of the Spirit is love. You know that God commands you genuinely to love him. And you know your inability to do what God requires.

Honesty demands that you confess your deficiency. Faith prompts you to trust God the Spirit to show His love for that person through you. Faith surrenders to the Holy Spirit's control and cooperates with His promptings. When you cooperate with the Spirit, you will be amazed to find a new freedom and power to reach out in service to that person through love (*Galatians 5:13*).

18 NOVEMBER

"Love never fails" (*1 Corinthians 13:8*).

Without love, Paul says, "I am nothing" and all I do "profits me nothing" (*1 Corinthians 13:2, 3*). With love your life inevitably counts for the glory of God. Love is the "more excellent way" (*1 Corinthians 12:31*).

If you read chapter 13 carefully you will notice that the personal pronoun "I" is found seven times in the first three verses. Then in the next four verses, which are a description of love, you will not find even one reference to the personal pronoun. Love is the absence of self. To the degree that self is still present, love is lacking.

It matters not whether you are eloquent in speech, can predict the future, know all mysteries, have faith strong enough to remove mountains, give all you possess to feed the poor, or even give your life as a martyr. If you don't love, it is all in vain.

That's why Paul encourages the Corinthians—and us—to "pursue love" (*1 Corinthians 14:1*). Jesus Christ perfectly fits the description of love in verses 4-7. Seek Him and ask Him to live His life through you. Then you will be able to love even as He loved.

19 NOVEMBER

"And let us consider how to stimulate one another to love and good deeds, not forsaking our own assembling together, as is the habit of some, but encouraging one another; and all the more, as you see the day drawing near" (Hebrews 10:24, 25).

Jesus Christ knows how much we need each other if we are to grow and be prepared for His return. Some Christians feel as though they don't need to attend church regularly. They are afraid churchgoing will become just a shallow habit. God knows better. He knows that no church is perfect. He also knows that interaction with imperfect people presents the challenge to love them and do good to them so that they will be stimulated to do the same. In this way we encourage one another.

It is far easier to slip into the habit of not assembling together with fellow Christians than it is to establish the discipline of assembling with them regularly. In the first century, Christians met together daily in the temple and from house to house (*Acts 2:46*). The writer of Hebrews encourages us to assemble "all the more, as you see the day drawing near." One characteristic of the end times is the busy lives so many of us lead. Busy, busy, busy doing many things, but often neglecting to our own loss the most important things in life. We must stop forsaking our assembling with other Christians if we want to be ready when Jesus Christ returns for His own.

20 NOVEMBER

ULTIMATE SUCCESS—2 CORINTHIANS
(four days to read)

"Therefore, we are ambassadors for Christ, as though God were entreating through us; we beg you on behalf of Christ, be reconciled to God" (2 Corinthians 5:20).

"It is better to fail in a cause that will ultimately succeed, than to succeed in a cause that will ultimately fail." These words of Peter Marshall represent the way Paul must have looked at his work for God. There were times when it seemed as though Paul had utterly failed, but the love of Christ constrained him to keep at it.

As you read Paul's autobiography in 2 Corinthians, see if you can find out how Paul went about his work. What was his message? What did he aim at in his ministry? What was his method? What were his thoughts about himself in relation to his work for God? Answers to these questions will help you understand God's purpose and place for you in advancing what will ultimately succeed.

21 NOVEMBER

"But I say: Love your enemies" (*Matthew 5:44, The Living Bible*).

David, the man after God's own heart, is seen in Psalm 69 struggling through a time of deep discouragement. In desperation he entreats God to take vengeance on his enemies (vv. 22-28). Then he asks God to bless him (vv. 29-36). David was right in asking God to take vengeance on his enemies, especially since his enemies were also the enemies of God. But the whole spirit of what he prayed seems foreign to Christ's instructions to love and pray for those who mistreat you (*Matthew 5:44*).

As Jesus Christ approached the cross, He was faced with circumstances similar to those of David. In fact David prophetically gives details of Christ's ordeal in Gethsemane and on the cross (vv. 20, 21). But how differently Christ reacted! He prayed, "Father, forgive these people . . . for they don't know what they are doing" (*Luke 23:34, The Living Bible*).

If you find yourself surrounded by oppressors and it seems impossible to follow the higher principles of Christ, then you might well pray as Thomas Fuller did, "Lord, please either lighten the load or strengthen my back." An African proverb says, "He who forgives ends the quarrel." Ask God to give you a forgiving heart toward those who have hurt you or made your way hard.

22 NOVEMBER

"But I say: Love your enemies" *(Matthew 5:44, The Living Bible).*

Jesus said, "There is a saying, 'Love your *friends* and hate your *enemies*' " (*Matthew 5:43, The Living Bible*). This is the natural attitude the human heart displays—love that which is desirable. Jesus, however, challenges you with the humanly impossible: "Love your *enemies*! Pray for those who persecute you!" God responds that way to man, "for he gives his sunlight to both the evil and the good, and sends rain on the just and on the unjust" (*Matthew 5:45*),*The Living Bible*). In this, God the Father manifests His perfection of character. As you walk in love toward your enemies you will become "imitators of God, as beloved children" (*Ephesians 5:1*).

The first step you can take in loving your enemy is to pray for him. From there God will guide you in taking the next step.

23 NOVEMBER

"As often as you eat this bread and drink the cup, you proclaim the Lord's death until He comes" (1 Corinthians 11:26).

Communion, or The Lord's Supper, was instituted by

Jesus Christ to be a unique reminder to us of the significance of His sacrificial death. It was to be a perpetual reminder, something that we experience with regularity. But there is more to Communion than looking back by faith to that which Christ has done for us on the cross. He told His disciples at the Last Supper that He would not drink of the fruit of the vine until He would drink it with them in the kingdom of God (*Matthew 26:29*). John refers to that future event in Revelation 19:1-10. When we partake of Communion, we should not forget to focus on this future event—the heart of our blessed hope.

It is interesting to note John's human error in worshiping the angel (v. 10). We, like John, when we try to worship aright are often distracted by our surroundings. In our minds the message, the messenger, his mannerisms, or the method employed in serving Communion may become more dominant than our Lord. We need to be reminded to "worship *God*!" Read Colossians 3:1-4 to enrich your meditation on this portion in the Revelation.

24 NOVEMBER

SPIRITUAL LIBERTY—GALATIANS
(two days to read)

"For you were called to freedom, brethren; only do not turn your freedom into an opportunity for the flesh, but through love serve one another" (Galatians 5:13).

In a zoo it is not a rare sight to see a caged hawk fan its wings in a vain attempt to break out of its prison. Hawks were created to soar in the limitless sky, not to exist in the narrow confines of those bars.

In Galatians Paul declares that we were created to enjoy spiritual liberty: freedom from legalism, license, and laziness; freedom which expresses itself in loving labor. We are saved to serve, liberated to labor, freed to "fulfill the law of Christ."

A few hundred years ago, God used the book of Galatians to transform the life of Martin Luther and through him the course of history. Let its message grip your life and set you free to be all God meant you to be.

25 NOVEMBER

"O how I love Thy law! It is my meditation all the day" (Psalm 119:97).

This is the declaration of a wise man. Devotion to the Word of God and dedication to its precepts is necessary for spiritual growth. But the Psalmist indicates it was not a matter of necessity. It was a matter of delight.

If you want to delight in the Word of God, you should make it your meditation all the day. The better you know God's Word, the more responsible you are to obey it. The more faithfully you obey it, the more you will love it. You will discover it to be trustworthy, beneficial, and relevant. And that in turn will encourage you to meditate in it the more.

26 NOVEMBER

SPIRITUAL LOVELINESS—EPHESIANS
(two days to read)

"Just as He chose us in Him before the foundation of the world, that we should be holy and blameless before Him" (Ephesians 1:4).

"My husband's life has been changed quite drastically since he received Jesus Christ as his Savior," said a young, nonbelieving wife to me recently. "And I like him far more the way he is now."

That's what God has in mind when He brings anyone into a new, spiritual relationship with Himself. He wants to make your life attractive. Take note of all He has provided for you as you read through Ephesians. Paul prays in this book that God will enlighten Christians to understand and then lead them into the experience of what they understand. Ask God to answer that prayer for you personally. And remember, spiritual loveliness is not something vague, sentimental, or merely emotional. It is not something we can put on at will. It is the product of God's workmanship within us.

27 NOVEMBER

"Having cleansed her [the Church] by the washing of water with the word" (*Ephesians 5:26*).

The Word of God is not only a protector against evil, it has the power to purge us from evil. Jesus said to His disciples, "You are already clean because of the word which I have spoken to you" (*John 15:3*).

In expounding this truth, Dr. William Culbertson once referred to one who took a woven basket down to a lake and scooped up a basket of water. By the time he got back to his cabin, all the water had leaked through the weaving. That's how it is with many of us when we try filling our minds with God's Word—it leaks out so fast we can't remember it. One thing is certain, however. The basket was cleaner after having carried the water, even though it wasn't able to retain the water. "Just so," he said, "when we allow the Word of God to enter our minds, we might think it merely seeps out and is forgotten. But the process purifies our minds."

It is a good discipline to take regular washings in the Word of God. That is one purpose God had in mind when He gave us His Word.

28 NOVEMBER

LIVING IN CHRIST—PHILIPPIANS
(one day to read)

"That I may know Him, and the power of His resurrection and the fellowship of His sufferings, being conformed to His death" (Philippians 3:10).

Corrie Ten Boom has observed that "if a bird is flying for pleasure it flies with the wind, but if it meets danger it turns and faces the wind, in order that it may rise higher." Paul often faced danger, even death; but like the bird, he was driven higher by adversity.

Philippians was written from a prison cell where Paul was facing the possibility of death for the cause of Christ. His attitude, however, and his concern for the well-being of other Christians is inspiring. And the insights he shares are well worth mastering.

You will see Christ in the life of Paul more in Philippians than in any other book he wrote—and that in fact is what he focuses on here: knowing Christ and making Him known at any cost.

29 NOVEMBER

CHRIST IS ALL IN ALL—COLOSSIANS
(one day to read)

"As you therefore have received Christ Jesus the Lord, so walk in Him" (Colossians 2:6).

Bobby Richardson, famous American athlete, manifested a clear understanding of the main practical principle of Colossians when in a large meeting he prayed pointedly, "Dear God, Your will, nothing more, nothing less, nothing else. Amen."

As you read Colossians you will see that Christ is Lord because He is the Creator of all. He is the only One who

can put real meaning into anyone's life. He is the only real
answer to everyone's quest for God. And He alone enables
men to relate to each other as they want to and should.
Either you let Him be Lord of all, or He is not Lord at all
in your life.

30 NOVEMBER

WHERE ARE YOU GOING?—1 THES-
SALONIANS (four days to read)

*"But let us who live in the light keep sober, protected by
the armor of faith and love, and wearing as our helmet the
happy hope of salvation. For God has not chosen to pour
out his anger upon us, but to save us through our Lord
Jesus Christ; he died for us so that we can live with him
forever, whether we are dead or alive at the time of his
return. So encourage each other to build each other up, just
as you are already doing"* (1 Thessalonians 5:8-11, The
Living Bible).

A godly old man was asked by a young Christian, "What
would you do if you knew that Jesus Christ was returning
tomorrow?" Expecting to be told that the old man would
feverishly go out into the streets and warn everyone to get
ready, he was surprised to hear him say, "I would go on
living as I have been living. I always seek to live as though
Christ were coming today."

As you read 1 Thessalonians you will discover that such a
life of security is encouraged for all. Such preparedness for
the future will always inspire and involve both service for
the Lord and sanctity of life. Walk worthily and work
watchfully while you wait for your Lord and Savior, Jesus
Christ. That kind of life knows where it is going. And it
will get there.

1 DECEMBER

"Wait for His Son from heaven"
(1 Thessalonians 1:10).

Another method for studying the Bible could be called the doctrinal or topical method. You begin by choosing a doctrine or topic and then listing all the references to it in a particular book or in the whole Bible. Use a concordance if you cover more than a particular book for your references. Make a note of all that those references have to say on the subject. Look for example at the references to Christ's return in 1 Thessalonians: 1:3, steadfast hope; 1:10, wait for Christ's return from heaven—Christ is the resurrected One who delivers us from the wrath to come; 2:19, 20, converts are Paul's glory and joy at Christ's return; (you fill in the details for the following) 3:13; 4:15-18; 5:1-11, 23. Once you have the facts, spread them out before you and group related truths together.

2 DECEMBER

"The coming of our Lord Jesus Christ"
(1 Thessalonians 5:23).

Give each group of facts a title. These titles become the main points in an outline. Use the facts themselves to develop subpoints under the main points.

For example, in 1 Thessalonians you might do a study of the doctrine of Christ's return, labeling some groups as follows:

1. Who is returning?
2. When will He return?
3. For whom will He return?
4. How can one prepare for His return?

Subpoints for the first question might work out like this:

a. Christ who is God's Son

b. Christ who is the resurrected one
c. Christ who is the deliverer from wrath
d. Christ who is the Lord
e. Christ who is the Savior

3 DECEMBER

"We shall always be with the Lord. Therefore comfort one another with these words"
(*1 Thessalonians 4:17, 18*).

Once you have developed a thorough outline, you can make some deductions and applications of the truth to your life. Based upon the material on Christ's return as presented in 1 Thessalonians, some personal applications might include the following:

1. If a loved one who is a believer dies, comfort can be found in affirming the promise of resurrection at Christ's return.

2. We should seek to win people to a trusting relationship with Christ as a preparation for His return. Persons I win to Christ will be my hope, joy, and crown of exultation. My responsibility to such persons, however, is not finished until they are established unblameable in holiness. That requires me to be everlastingly at my task. (Note chapters 2 and 3.)

4 DECEMBER

OPPOSING LAWLESSNESS—2 THESSALONIANS (one day to read)
"With all these things in mind, dear brothers, stand firm and keep a strong grip on the truth that we taught you in our letters and during the time we were with you"
(*2 Thessalonians 2:15, The Living Bible*).

Lawlessness actually is a misnomer. Laws operate whether we accept them or not. When we think we have overcome or evaded a given law, we merely discover another taking its place. Our universe functions according to law and order.

Pastor-author Ray Ortlund once confided, "As a boy I once ran head-on into a barbed-wire fence. The fence wasn't hurt, but I was! I still bear the scars of that experience. You can't tangle with barbed-wire fences and get by with it."

You can't disregard the law of God either without facing bitter consequences. As you read 2 Thessalonians, note the following instructions on this theme: be assured that in the end God will punish lawlessness; be aware that until the end God is permitting lawlessness within limits; be involved until the end in opposing any practice of lawlessness. We should live in harmony with God's established order, or it will order us to the hell of eternal destruction from the presence of God.

5 DECEMBER

THE SERVANT'S LESSON-BOOK—
1 TIMOTHY (one day to read)

"Put these abilities to work; throw yourself into your tasks so that everyone may notice your improvement and progress. Keep a close watch on all you do and think. Stay true to what is right and God will bless you and use you to help others" (1 Timothy 4:15, 16, The Living Bible).

If you are a Christian and you want to serve the Lord, but you're not sure how to go about it, then read 1 Timothy with care. Paul, who wrote the book, was an experienced servant of the Lord. He knew the answers to the kind of questions young Timothy had as he went out to serve the Lord. Many of your questions will be answered too. And very likely some issues you did not consider important will also be explained with proper emphasis.

Paul makes it clear that to serve others you must maintain a growing relationship with the Lord yourself. You can't lead others beyond where you are. Be an example; then exhort and encourage others in the ways of God. And don't let anything discourage you from continuing in your work. Kaj Munk, a fiery Danish minister, refused to get deviated from his calling to preach the gospel. He challenges others: "Let us give up being great in little things and be great in the great."

6 DECEMBER

A SOLDIER'S LEGACY—2 TIMOTHY
(one day to read)

"Take your share of suffering as a good soldier of Jesus Christ, just as I do, and as Christ's soldier do not let yourself become tied up in worldly affairs, for then you cannot satisfy the one who has enlisted you in his army" (2 Timothy 2:3, 4, The Living Bible).

Paul had fought a good fight, run a good race, and kept the faith. Now that it was time for him to die he placed his mantle on his protegeᴅ, young Timothy. The road ahead was tough. Paul warned Timothy of the difficulties and dangers. But he also shared the secrets to success he had discovered while in his spiritual battles for the Lord.

To fight successfully, Paul maintained, requires fearlessness. It also requires faithfulness. Furthermore, it requires freedom from entanglements. Your reward for such sacrificial service might be the loss of all things valued by the world. But Paul would agree with Jim Elliot who was martyred along with four other missionaries as they attempted to take the gospel to the Aucas. As a perceptive young man Jim Elliot wrote, "He is no fool who gives what he cannot keep to gain what he cannot lose."

7 DECEMBER

SPIRITUAL LEADERSHIP—TITUS
(one day to read)

"In all things show yourself to be an example of good deeds, with purity in doctrine, dignified, sound in speech which is beyond reproach, in order that the opponent may be put to shame, having nothing bad to say about us" (*Titus 2:7, 8*).

D. L. Moody was once confronted with the challenge of a friend who said, "The world has yet to see what God can do with a man wholly yielded to God." To himself Moody made the vow, "By the grace of God, I will be that man." Only God knows the total impact Moody's life made upon the world.

God has always looked for men and women totally yielded to Him, for one man can do far more in submission to God than any number of men can do without submission to God.

In Titus you will find a standard test to discover such spiritual leaders. See if you can make up a list of qualifications from the book. Then make up a list of guidelines for those who are spiritual leaders which might help them fulfill their task in a way which would please God.

8 DECEMBER

ARE YOU AVAILABLE?—PHILEMON
(one day to read)

"I've written you this letter because I am positive that you will do what I ask and even more" (*Philemon 21, The Living Bible*).

Well has it been said: "The Lord looks not for ability, nor for inability, but for availability." You will see this beautifully illustrated when you read Philemon.

As Philemon's slave, Onesimus was not ready to accept Philemon's Christianity. He might once have said, "If I was rich like him, then I'd become a Christian too." But when Onesimus became a runaway slave, God led him to Paul, who was in prison. There, circumstances showed him that Christianity was not for the privileged only. It was also for forgottens, such as prisoners and slaves. Paul, who was available to God in prison, won Onesimus to the Savior.

As Onesimus made himself available to God, he became profitable to Paul. But Paul felt obligated to send him back to Philemon his master. Paul was confident he would also be profitable there now. He wrote this short letter to encourage Philemon to make himself available as an instrument in the hands of God, lovingly accepting and helping the young convert.

Availability is the name of the game.

9 DECEMBER

LOOK TO JESUS CHRIST—HEBREWS
(five days to read)

"Hence, also, He is able to save forever those who draw near to God through Him, since He always lives to make intercession for them" (Hebrews 7:25).

Is it not arrogance for Christians to say, "Jesus Christ is the Light of the world"? Or to say, "Only we have the light"? Dr. Radhakrishnan, the Hindu philosopher who became president of India, paused for a moment to ponder these questions. Then he replied, "Yes, but the Christian has no choice. This is what your Scriptures say; you cannot say less. You are saved from arrogance when you say it in the spirit of Jesus Christ."

The book of Hebrews declares that Jesus Christ is the substance of all that the Old Testament pre-shadowed. He is superior to all who have gone before or who will come after Him. His provision of salvation is alone adequate to meet our deepest needs. It is therefore reasonable and essential to look to Jesus Christ and believe on Him with all our heart and soul and mind.

10 DECEMBER

"We must pay much closer attention to what we have heard" (Hebrews 2:1).

Another method of Bible study is what we'll call the analytical approach. In this method you start with the details and work toward the unifying theme. It is the opposite of the synthetic approach where you start with the main theme and work from it down to the details. You might understand it better if you imagine yourself starting to work on a picture puzzle. When you have removed all the puzzle pieces from the box, you then spread them all out before you. You see to it that all the pieces are right side up. Then you look for similar colors and place them together in groups. Next you put pieces together within the groups. And finally you put the groups together, filling in connecting pieces as necessary. This is similar to the procedure used in this approach to Bible study. We'll use Hebrews 2:1-4 as an example.

11 DECEMBER

"The word spoken through angels proved unalterable" (Hebrews 2:2).

Try spreading out the pieces of truth found in Hebrews 2:1-4.

Verse 1: We have a reason for the challenge given. We are

accountable to Christ, who as God is more important than angels or prophets. Some attention has been given to what was heard of God's Word (likely New Testament truth), but much closer attention ought to be given to it. There is a danger of drifting from what we know is His will, or drifting past the truth.

Verse 2: In the Old Testament God at times spoke through angels. What they said proved unalterable. Transgression means one has stepped over a line. Disobedience indicates one has neglected to hear and therefore has not followed God's will. For either reason, punishment is inevitable.

Now, you do the same for verses 3 and 4.

12 DECEMBER

"How shall we escape, if we neglect so great salvation?" (Hebrews 2:3).

Once you have spread out the facts as indicated yesterday, you put similar things together in groups. Three possible groups into which you might place the facts you find in Hebrews 2:1-4 are:

1. Reasons why we should not neglect God's Word
2. Ways in which some do neglect God's Word
3. Consequences when one neglects God's Word

13 DECEMBER

"So great a salvation . . . spoken by the Lord" (Hebrews 2:3).

Under the title for each group you should be able to list some supporting points. For example, under *Reasons*

why we should not neglect God's Word, you might list the
following points:

a. Old Testament truth *proved* to be unalterable as seen
in just recompence where necessary.

b. New Testament truth was given personally by the
Lord, who is greater than agents through whom the Old
Testament was given.

c. New Testament truth was confirmed through attesting
signs determined by God.

Now list some supporting points under the other group
titles. When you have done this, you essentially have an
outline of the material studied. To complete the study, state
your conclusion as the overall theme or title. For example:
*God's Word is trustworthy; to neglect it is folly; to heed it
brings great gain.* All that is necessary now is to translate
your conclusion into personal application.

14 DECEMBER

DOERS OF THE WORD—JAMES
(two days to read)

*"But one who looks intently at the perfect law, the law of
liberty, and abides by it, not having become a forgetful
hearer but an effectual doer, this man shall be blessed in
what he does"* (James 1:25).

As you read James you will recognize its similarity to
Proverbs in the Old Testament. It is as much concerned
with our behavior as with our belief.

James focuses on some areas of behavior that are common
weak spots in the lives of Christians. He shows how to cope
with them. His main argument is that "faith without works

is dead." Dr. Alan Redpath was once accused of preaching a gospel of works. He replied, "I don't preach a gospel of works. I preach a gospel that works." Faith which does not transform the life is dead faith.

"Is the message done?" someone asked another who returned from a church service sooner than usual.

"No, not yet," was the reply. "It is preached, but it still remains to be done."

15 DECEMBER

"Consider it all joy, my brethren, when you encounter various trials" (James 1:2).

A simpler method of Bible study than those previously considered consists of answering questions. Read James 1:12-16 and answer the following questions:

1. What do you learn about God (or Christ or the Holy Spirit)?
2. What do you learn about man?
3. What promise(s) can you claim?
4. What warning(s) should you heed?
5. What is the key verse and theme?

Following are some suggested answers which you can compare with the ones you came up with:

1. God cannot be tempted with evil.
2. Man has the potential of being tempted by evil because of lust.
3. God will reward those victorious over temptation.
4. Don't play with temptation, for it can lead to sin and death—resist it right away. And don't blame God when you are tempted.

5. Verse 16. When tempted to do evil, resist by acknowledging your own weakness, and by trusting in God for victory. He's on your side.

16 DECEMBER

THE SUFFERER'S REWARD—1 PETER
(two days to read)

"Dear friends, don't be bewildered or surprised when you go through the fiery trials ahead, for this is no strange, unusual thing that is going to happen to you. Instead, be really glad—because these trials will make you partners with Christ in his suffering, and afterwards you will have the wonderful joy of sharing his glory in that coming day when it will be displayed" (1 Peter 4:12, 13, The Living Bible).

On his first furlough as a missionary from Africa, Charles McCleary said to friends, "When a bridge is built, some foundation stones must be laid beneath the water. If God wills that I should be one of the deep stones to build the bridge in Africa, and I must be buried there, I am ready." Six months later he died, but his work lived on. His wife stayed on and guided a tremendous ministry.

Jesus Christ our Savior suffered much. His life was filled with pain. Yet He remained true to His heavenly Father and to His calling, "leaving us an example, that you should follow His steps"(1 Peter 2:21).

If we follow Christ closely, suffering will be inevitable. God promised it, so don't be surprised when it comes. Accept the fact that God has a purpose in our suffering. It sanctifies our faith. It brings us to the place of surrender and trust. Many times it is the only route to spiritual maturity.

When danger and suffering confront you, remember what pioneer missionary J. Hudson Taylor wrote: "The greatest mission is submission."

17 DECEMBER

"Like newborn babes, long for the pure milk of the word, that by it you may grow in respect to salvation" (1 Peter 2:2).

One final method of Bible study would be to use the following points to help you dissect a portion of Scripture: give it a title, select a key verse, state the most significant truth, list any cross-references you know, note any difficulties, develop some applications to life, and then summarize or outline the material.

Always remember, it is not as important how much of the Bible you know as how much of the Bible has become a part of your life experience. Prayer is important as you prepare for study, as well as when you apply what you have learned. Dependence upon the Holy Spirit as your Teacher and Enabler is also necessary.

18 DECEMBER

THE SAVIOR'S LONGSUFFERING—
2 PETER (one day to read)

"The Lord is not slow about His promise, as some count slowness, but is patient toward you, not wishing for any to perish but for all to come to repentance" (2 Peter 3:9).

Robert Moffat understood the reason for the Savior's longsuffering. He exhorts us, "We have all eternity to celebrate our victories, but only one short hour before sunset in which to win them."

As you read 2 Peter you will be impressed with the fact that when God makes a promise He always keeps it. Nothing can stop Him. When He is satisfied that the best time for fulfillment has arrived, it will come to pass. This is true in regard to Christ's return. In the fullness of time He will come.

Until that day, "regard the patience of our Lord to be

salvation" (*2 Peter 3:15*). You cannot afford to presume upon it or play with it. If you do, you will surely suffer bad consequences. You should be grateful for His longsuffering and use the extra time to diligently prepare yourself and persuade others to prepare themselves for the day of the Lord.

19 DECEMBER

CHRISTIAN LOVE—1 JOHN
(two days to read).

"And this commandment we have from Him, that the one who loves God should love his brother also" (*1 John 4:21*).

John's motto for life was the Lord's commandment that if you love God, you should also love your brother. He was concerned, as James was, with the tangible expression of love to God. And more than that, he knew all men are starving for someone to really love them. Victor Hugo indicates this when he says, "The supreme happiness of life is the conviction that we are loved."

The problem is that many don't know of God's love for them, nor will they believe it to be true until they experience it through the life of one of God's children. First-century Christians were known for their love to one another. May we be known by such love too. As you read 1 John, note the qualities of this love explained and illustrated.

20 DECEMBER

"Every spirit that does not confess Jesus is not from God; and this is the spirit of the antichrist, of which you have heard that it is coming, and now it is already in the world" (*1 John 4:3*).

There are those who feel we don't need to worry about the spirit of antichrist, because the antichrist will rise to prominence during the tribulation which takes place after the Church has been raptured and is with the Lord. I myself hold the view that the Church will not be here on earth when the antichrist rises to prominence. However, John says that the *spirit* of antichrist is *any spirit that does not confess Jesus.* He points out that his readers have heard that this spirit of antichrist is coming. He continues by declaring, "and now it is already in the world." That was in the first century!

When you read church history, it is unmistakable that the spirit of antichrist has been very much present in every age. And it is very prevalent today. In fact, there is much evidence to indicate the spirit of antichrist is in ascendance. Paul says, "For the mystery of lawlessness is already at work; only he who now restrains will do so until he is taken out of the way. And then that lawless one will be revealed whom the Lord will slay with the breath of His mouth and bring to an end by the appearance of His coming" (*2 Thessalonians 2:7, 8*).

21 DECEMBER

LOVE IS OBEDIENCE—2 JOHN
(one day to read)

"If we love God, we will do whatever he tells us to. And he has told us from the very first to love each other" (*2 John 6, The Living Bible*).

If Christians were to be guided by just one principle, that principle should be "that we love one another." In a real sense, love fulfills the whole law. It enables one to fulfill the law not grudgingly or of necessity, but gladly.

To love God means that we obey Him in every detail of His will for us. We prove and portray our love by obeying. As a child's obedience makes merry the heart of his parents, so obedience to God makes Him glad.

True love is also jealous. Jealous for the honor of the one loved. If we truly love the Lord Jesus Christ, we will be jealous for His honor. Compromise with what is contrary to God's will leads inevitably to catastrophe in the Christian life. Never take a chance about this!

22 DECEMBER

AGAINST SELF-LOVE—3 JOHN
(one day to read)

"Beloved, do not imitate what is evil, but what is good. The one who does good is of God; the one who does evil has not seen God" (3 John 11).

There is a healthy love of self, for Jesus Christ tells us to love our neighbor as ourselves (*Matthew 22:39*). Excessive love of self, however, is destructive to the Christian life and to the Christian Church. Everyone knows this, yet many are ensnared in its web.

Tradition tells us that David kept a shepherd's staff beside his throne to remind him of his humble service as a shepherd, from which he had been exalted to become king over his people. Diotrephes was not like David. Diotrephes, of whom John wrote in this brief epistle, loved the preeminence among the Christians. As you read this letter, note John's strong condemnation of that kind of self-love and his challenge to become not like Diotrephes but like Demetrius, who had "a good report of all men."

23 DECEMBER

SANCTIFIED OR LUKEWARM—JUDE
(one day to read)

"Beloved, while I was making every effort to write you

*about our common salvation, I felt the necessity to write to
you appealing that you contend earnestly for the faith
which was once for all delivered to the saints" (Jude 3).*

Spurgeon once warned, "Error oft rides to its deadly work
on the back of truth." As you read Jude you will see how
this in fact happens within a church. You will also see how
it is to be handled.

Jude warns against the lukewarm who "turn the grace of
God into lasciviousness" (v. 4). Then he describes their
ultimate doom. Christians are to be careful that they are not
led astray from the faith they have entered. Yet they are to
reach out to those outside the faith, desiring to snatch them
from judgment. God promises to keep them in their venture
for Him.

24 DECEMBER

*"For a child will be born to us, a son will be
given to us; and the government will rest on
His shoulders; and His name will be called . . . Prince of
Peace" (Isaiah 9:6, 7).*

The world searches for peace. One political leader after
another promises peace, but all fail to deliver it. Jesus
Christ, the promised child to be born, son to be given, came
into this world to bring peace. The angels announced to the
shepherds, "Glory to God in the highest, and on earth
peace among men with whom He is pleased" (Luke 2:14).

Sadly, not many responded to the arrival of Jesus Christ
in the way God wanted them to. Consequently there has
been only limited peace on the earth over the past two
millennia. But the Prince of Peace, who was rejected by
His own people when He came to them the first time, is
coming again.

Before His return, cataclysmic events will occur in the
political, social, and physical world. The unveiling of the
antichrist and all who follow him will lead to the

ultimate revolt against God at Armageddon. Christ will return to overthrow all opposition and establish His kingdom in which peace will prevail. His archenemy, Satan, will be bound and cast into the bottomless pit so that he cannot thwart the peace program of Christ's kingdom (*Revelation 20:1-3*). And even after the 1,000-year reign of Christ on earth, the revolt of Gog and Magog will interrupt that eternal peace for a brief moment.

The peace we can know personally and corporately within the church is but a foretaste of the eternal peace that God is preparing for His own.

25 DECEMBER

A FINAL RECKONING!—THE REVELATION (seven days to read)

"Worthy art Thou, our Lord and our God, to receive glory and honor and power; for Thou didst create all things, and because of Thy will they existed, and were created" (*Revelation 4:11*).

You must know the man who said, "We shall go on to the end . . . we shall never surrender," before you can really understand England's part in World War 2. For it was Sir Winston Churchill's determination, courage, and statesmanship which brought victory to England when defeat seemed almost certain.

Likewise, you must know the Sovereign Lord who dominates the scenes of The Revelation if you are to understand the events foretold therein. As you read this final book of the Bible, you will see Jesus Christ as the Sovereign Lord of time as well as of the Church. He is also the Sovereign Lord of heaven, of earth, and of eternity.

Modern man trifles with time, cares little about the Church, is humorous about heaven, pollutes the earth, and tries to ignore eternity. But there is coming a day when we must stand alone before the Sovereign Lord of all. On that day there will be no more trifling, heedlessness, joking, carelessness, or evading. Therefore, let us prepare to meet our Sovereign Lord by surrendering to Him now and serving Him to the end.

26 DECEMBER

"The Lord is our God, the Lord is one!"
(Deuteronomy 6:4).

The Hebrew word translated *one* in this and other verses refers to a compound unity, not a simple unity. God refers to marriage as two people becoming "one" flesh (*Genesis 2:24*). He refers to the people who built the tower of Babel as being "one" people (*Genesis 11:6*). The "one" found in these verses is not the numerical digit "1" in the series of numbers 1, 2, 3, 4, 5. Rather, it refers to a state of unity. God is a unified Being.

"To you it was shown that you might know that the Lord, He is God; there is no other besides Him" (*Deuteronomy 4:35*). "Thus says the Lord . . . there is no God besides Me" (*Isaiah 44:6*). When asked which commandment is the foremost of all, Jesus answered, "The foremost is, 'Hear, O Israel; the Lord our God is one Lord; and you shall love the Lord your God with all your heart, and with all your soul, and with all your mind, and with all your strength'" (*Mark 12:29, 30*).

27 DECEMBER

"For yet in a very little while, He who is coming will come, and will not delay"
(Hebrews 10:37).

Even in the first century, Christians were encouraged to be prepared for the imminent (close at hand) return of Jesus

Christ. They were not to be slack concerning their work for the Savior. They were to be ready for the Lord when He comes. How much more should we in these latter days walk in this manner!

Prophecy has been fulfilled remarkably in our generation. Israel is again in her land and in possession of Jerusalem. World powers are being aligned as predicted by God's prophets. Turmoil and uncertainty are spreading throughout the world. We should not be asleep, but alert and sober. "That day of the Lord will come unexpectedly like a thief in the night. When people are saying, 'All is well, everything is quiet and peaceful'—then, all of a sudden, disaster will fall upon them as suddenly as a woman's birth pains begin when her child is born. And these people will not be able to get away anywhere—there will be no place to hide . . . God has not chosen to pour out his anger upon us, but to save us through our Lord Jesus Christ . . . So encourage each other to build each other up" (1 Thessalonians 5:2, 3, 9, 11, The Living Bible).

John, in writing about this glorious event, concludes, "And every one who has this hope fixed on Him [Jesus Christ] purifies himself, just as He is pure" (1 John 3:3).

28 DECEMBER

"[God] isn't really being slow about his promised return, even though it sometimes seems that way. But he is waiting, for the good reason that he is not willing that any should perish, and he is giving more time for sinners to repent. The day of the Lord is surely coming, as unexpectedly as a thief" (2 Peter 3:9, 10, The Living Bible).

There are those who feel that talk about the imminent return of Jesus Christ is nothing more than alarmism. Things really haven't changed that much, they feel. Peter predicted, "In the last days there will come scoffers who will do every wrong they can think of, and laugh at the truth. This will be their line of argument: 'So Jesus promised to come back, did he? Then where is he? He'll never come! Why, as far back as anyone can remember everything has remained exactly as it was since the first day of creation'" (2 Peter 3:3, 4, The Living Bible).

Rather than becoming calloused towards others, we should be patient, as the Lord is. Christ died so that all sinners might be saved. God does not wish for anyone to perish in a Christless eternity. He wishes for all to come to repentance. He is, therefore, extending the time of opportunity to give more an opportunity to come into His saving grace.

Should we not use this extra time to buy up each opportunity for spreading the good news far and wide? Dare we take the luxury of sitting back and waiting for people to come to us? We must go to the people where they are and proclaim the Lord to them. The day of the Lord is coming. When it comes, it will overtake the unwary and the unprepared as a thief. Then it will be too late. What we do for Jesus must be done now!

29 DECEMBER

"Pray much for others; plead for God's mercy upon them; give thanks for all he is going to do for them. Pray in this way for kings and all others who are in authority over us . . ." (1 Timothy 2: 1, 2, The Living Bible).

Many times in our earthly pilgrimage those in authority over us may try to lead us in a direction away from God and His will. In some countries that may occur *most* of the time. We might not think there is much we can do about it. But we can! We can always pray. In fact, we are commanded to. And when we do pray in faith for those over us, we should not be surprised to see God answer. Be specific in your prayers for your leaders. Don't just pray, "God bless them."

Some government leaders are godly. They need our prayers especially, that God would give them the wisdom and courage to continue doing what is right and to extend their influence on others.

We also are encouraged to pray for the peace of Jerusalem, because when God answers that prayer all will be well on the world scene.

30 DECEMBER

"If I regard wickedness in my heart, the Lord will not hear" (Psalm 66:18).

Prayer is an act of the heart in which by faith a person enters into God's holy presence to commune and communicate with Him. It is a conscious and deliberate act. The person knows with whom he is communicating. Therefore, he is responsible to prepare himself to come with the proper credentials.

What are those credentials? The most basic one is a clean heart. When the Psalmist says "regard," he means "to aim at, design something, or have it in mind." If I plan to do evil and in that state of mind come to the Lord in prayer, He will not listen to it. Such praying is sheer hypocrisy. God hears a prayer that comes from a heart and mind sincerely directed toward Him and His will.

Other credentials are humility *(Psalm 51:17)* and faith *(Hebrews 11:6; James 1:5-7)*. We must also take care to ask for things which are in harmony with His will *(1 John 5:14, 15)*. Finally, we must remember what is confidently declared in Hebrews 10:19-22.

31 DECEMBER

"Test yourselves to see if you are in the faith; examine yourselves!" (2 Corinthians 13:5).

As we come to the close of this "truth journey" through the Bible, it is wise to reflect for a moment. Has this study been profitable? Could it have been more profitable? How?

Yes, we are to examine ourselves and our own work (*Galatians 6:4*). Did you through your study and reading get to know God the Father, Son, and Holy Spirit better? Do you understand yourself, your enemy Satan, and the nature of the Church better? Have you learned how to study the Bible more effectively? In preparing this meditation manual these were some of my objectives.

I pray that you have grown in mind and heart "to a mature man, to the measure of the stature which belongs to the fulness of Christ" (*Ephesians 4:13*). As a result, I trust you will no longer be "tossed here and there by waves, and carried about by every wind of doctrine" (*Ephesians 4:14*). May God enable you to know, live, and share the truth in a greater way in each of your tomorrows until we meet in glory.

APR 1 5			